Exploring
Edges

Field Notes From Experiments in Medicine,
Endurance Sports, and Love

Travis A. Stephensen

TRAVIS A. STEPHENSEN

ISBN-10: 1518689310
ISBN-13: 978-1518689314

DEDICATION

This book is dedicated to:

My father, who taught me that I should do hard things because life is hard.

My wife Katie, who taught me to be gentle with myself because life is hard.

CONTENTS

ACKNOWLEDGEMENT

I would like to thank Brent Smith and Damara "Mergy" Simmons, for their invaluable editorial assistance.

Brent is one of those rare people who listens with great stillness, and speaks with great wisdom. The light of his brilliant mind illuminated wrinkles in the pages I could not see by myself.

Damara invested countless hours scrutinizing the pages and teaching me to tighten sentences until they were in tune. As she has always done, Mergy believed in me and pushed me to think, write and be better that I thought I was capable of. I am grateful for "that." *wink*

I would also like to thank my son Kasen for designing the cover. I have always had a fascination with names and words. I designed the name Kasen from making a list of all my favorite names and trying to recognize the best letter and sound combinations and iterating toward the best. Later I learned the Japanese word, "Kaizen" which means, "gradual improvement toward perfection." It's a perfect word to describe the origins of his name, how he designed the cover of this book, and how he lives his life.

*Traveling—first it leaves you speechless,
then it turns you into a story-teller.*
Ibn Battuta, Explorer

*I promise if you keep searching for everything beautiful
in this world you will eventually become it.*
Tyler Kent White, Poet

Mile 0.22

Vagary: (Latin) (n) an unpredictable instance; a wandering journey; a whimsical, wild, or unusual idea, desire, or action.

When I was eight years old I asked my dad if there were any blank spaces left on the maps, any islands or places that had not yet been discovered or explored. Without looking up from his *National Geographic*, my father absently told me no. I slouched back to my room confused. Though I had never known him to be wrong, this time I needed my father to be. If he wasn't, then my Heavenly Father had made a mistake and I had been born too late. Neither possibility made sense.

I loved reading about explorers and scientists and discovery. I loved reading about their leather travel journals filled with orange sand, notes, experiments, sepia sketches of new plants and animals, and newly discovered unanswered questions. I loved their impossibly long and dangerous journeys from which they returned changed: wiser, stronger and better. By traveling far geographically, they didn't just pass through the miles and leagues, but the miles and leagues passed through them and changed them. Mountaineers wrote that it was not the mountains they conquered—the mountains were unchanged—but the mountains of weaknesses in themselves had been conquered. Many times they met women along the way, and their love stories were also epics. The great heroes of sports pushed their bodies and their minds against their limits and redefined those boundaries for everyone. The nearly insurmountable challenges, the physical and mental exhaustion they faced didn't build their character; they simply served as tools that were hard enough to scratch away the weakness and reveal the solid truth about themselves that was hiding within. I didn't ache to be an explorer simply to know other places; I wanted to know myself. My father's news left me feeling the soul sadness of unrequited love.

I could not understand why something deep inside was attracting me to something that felt so right only to be told no. Books pressed my face up against the bars of my horrifyingly *normal* life and showed me what greatness looked like. I felt as though I was not allowed to be who I was put on earth to be: an adventurer. I remember looking up from my books and staring out the window at the old tire swing, and the clock-like tick of our sprinklers and mourning. All the great adventures were finished. All the great scientists, heroes, and explorers had already passed. All the great experiments and discoveries had already been made. All the great inventions had already been made. All that was left for me was the janitorial work of tidying up a few loose ends.

Slowly, almost out of the corner of my eye, I noticed something curious about heroes in the books I read: any times they were doing something else when they received their call to adventure, and although those other jobs initially seemed unrelated, they inevitably came in handy. C.S. Lewis wrote,

"Affliction is often that thing which prepares an ordinary person for some sort of extraordinary destiny." So, I made three vows: First, "I will prepare, and when adventure knocks, the door will swing open easily because I left it cracked and oiled." Second, I vowed to learn the rules of an adventurer. And lastly, I vowed that if I ever had an adventure, I would tell the story. I had noticed that many times the simple act of telling the story transformed it from "real life" into something larger, something surreal, metaphorical and mythical. Wonder and many times even magic bloomed from within the explorer, not just the exploration. G.K. Chesterton said, "We are perishing for want of wonder, not for want of wonders." People who wrote books were able to see and describe things that other people couldn't. The optics of their inquisitive eyes had lenses with a prescription for seeing and describing wonders. The act of telling their story was a way of planting a little flag and claiming an undiscovered piece of the world.

It took me thirty seven years to discover one area that I was called to explore. It took years to develop the necessary skills and confidence to even dare try. It took years to learn what was known, and where the blank spots on the map of human knowledge still existed. I went to medical school and learned what was known of the body. I listened carefully to patients talking about *pain* for years and spent hours and days and weeks thinking about what that word really meant. It took years of learning about myself to discover where the blank spots of my own self-knowledge existed. And it took years of thinking about why God or the Universe had summoned me here, into existence in the first place.

Instead of exploring the edges of a geographic map, or the blank spaces on it, I decided to be the exploring cartographer of the uncharted edges of my own body's physical limits and the unexplored blank spaces of my own mind and will. Like my heroes, this would be done via epic journeys, quests, and endurance *expeditions*. It took uncomfortably long trips to reach those edges, those borderlands, but it was invigorating to conduct experiments and to discover new things. Other people had explored the limits of *their* bodies. I would be the first and the only explorer in history to explore mine. It was an uncharted jungle, filled with puzzling relics from my ancestors, valuable artifacts, unusual foods, and hidden tribes with curious customs. Unexpected guides materialized, insisting on jobs for themselves where they could better conspire to help me with these explorations. I made discoveries; some areas of the maps of reality that I had been given by my family and my society were completely wrong, and required cartographic correction.

The fulcrum for many of these events was the marathon. As I read and prepared I learned that cartographers had struggled with the precise length of a marathon. It too had required cartographic correction. During the era of the modern Olympics from 1896 to 1920 the distance varied each time. Finally, it was decided to canonize the distance used at the 1908 London Olympics. At that time, a single lap at White City Stadium was added to the twenty-six mile course to finish in front of the Royal Box. This made it 26.22 miles. All those other twenty six miles were the invisible mass of the iceberg. But there was something wonderful about that final visible lap, that 0.22 mile. It was so logically arbitrary. It was an imperfection on the nose of twenty-six whole miles and yet this wart was the lap the public saw. It was the one of royal significance.

As I set out to explore, my self-doubts—my most faithful traveling companions—regularly reminded me that because I was unlikely to break the world records for these events, I did not have anything new or useful to say. I kept pressing forward into the unknown, hoping for an answer to that painfully valid point. Mile by mile, I discovered it. My self-doubts were partially correct: I did not set any time records. But I discovered that there is more than one way to measure these events than simply with units of distance and time. They can be measured in the non-metric units of: new insights, new smells, breathtaking sights, new friends made, insecurities overcome, experiments conducted, animals seen, people inspired, etceta. I could celebrate finish lines instead of finish times.

This book is the result of thoughts, conversations, and experiments I had with myself as I traveled hundreds and hundreds of miles. I thought about how to describe what I was feeling. I thought about why I was doing this, and how to explain it. Mile after mile I wrote this book in my head, netting the rare and fleeting insights after each run like a lepidopterist and then pinning them down in my field notes to be organized later. This book is the compilation and summary of my field notes.

What I wasn't expecting as I began these experiments was that they would follow the Heisenberg Uncertainty Principle, where the act of measuring something changes the behavior of the thing being measured. In this case, I was measuring myself, and I was not prepared for the incredible changes that action would have on my own life. Martin Buber once warned, "All journeys have secret destinations of which the traveler is unaware."

As I trained I also imagined you, curious reader, holding this book of my secrets in your clever hands, seeing the final lap in the stadium, weighing each word on the scales of your fiery mind. Mile after mile, I drew strength imagining telling you this crazy tale. If it speaks to you, and you find yourself wondering if I wrote this for you, the answer is: Yes, yes I did.

No parent can child-proof the world.
A parent's job is world-proof the child.
Doug Flanders, Physician

The legacy of Heroes is the memory of a great name
and the inheritance of a great example.
Benjamin Disraeli, Prime Minister

MILE 1
Son of a Run

Oriflamme. (Middle English) (n) a symbol or standard that inspires confidence, devotion, or courage.

Parents tell their kids stories. And sometimes kids tell themselves stories about those stories. My father put a heavy weight on me when I was four years old. It was the weight of who he expected me to be. After all the competing memories were scavenged for parts, it remains now as my earliest memory. It survives while so many other memories have washed away because of the intensity of the sadness in my father's eyes. Somehow sadness made it durable.

He summoned me to an empty room. I can't remember which one. The door knob clicked closed behind me, always an ominous sign. He was a giant. He sat in a chair. I stood before him, looking down. Leaning forward, my father put his warm, heavy hands on my shoulders. They engulfed my arms down to the elbows.

"Son, my dad told me something very important when I was a little boy." He paused, looking down, "And now I am going to tell you."

I looked at the floor also. When our eyes met, his eyes had the sad sparkle of broken glass.

"Travis, I expect you to be a better man than I have been. Will you do that?"

The weight of his hand on my shoulder was nothing compared to the weight of what he was asking of me. My father was a giant, a god! I was just a little boy.

How could I meet that impossible expectation?

I remember crying with the weight of the impossibility of his request. And then I remember being embarrassed that I was crying; maybe my tears were a warning of weakness that I would fail. But if his father had asked it of him, perhaps it was an ancient family charge. How many generations of my father's fathers had put the weight of their mighty hands, and this unattainable assignment on their little sons' shoulders? I wiped my nose on my sleeve and told my father I would try.

So, here was the family yoke, the family duty: a mission to not simply meet my father's impossible legacy, but to somehow exceed it. He had charged me with leading a munificent mutiny against himself, and to help me he would teach me how to do it by setting an example of what the life of a good man looked like. As I studied him, with the blinking, squinting scrutiny that children reserve for their parents, I tried to understand what made a good man and a good life. He wasn't going to simply hold still and wait for me. He raced ahead of me, making it even more impossible. My father was ravenous in his quest to improve and to grow. That this same expectation was extended to his children was a logical addition. Though his example and legacy were targets in perpetual motion, he left clues about what was important.

The philosophy behind this quest for improvement permeated everything he did. He conveyed his life philosophy by way of axioms he repeated over and over in dozens of different situations to show their universal applicability. Among these was, "You can tell what someone loves by how they spend their time, and how they spend their money." Sometimes he would rephrase it, "Children spell love: T-I-M-E." Or, as Marcus Aurelius put it, "The true worth of a man is to be measured by the objects he pursues."

And so I watched to see where my father spent his time so that I could know what was important. My father spent his time exercising and praying, studying and playing, soldiering and traveling. Most of the time I couldn't figure out where one ended and the next began. When he played with us it was in the form of exercise. When he went to work he reminded us to say our prayers at night. As a soldier he was always studying and exercising; sometimes at the same time. He gathered us together for family prayers before and after his military trips. Sometimes as we solemnly knelt in a circle for family prayer before bedtime, someone would start laughing quietly, and the harder we tried to be reverent, the harder it became to hold our laughter. My father warned us this lack of reverence was disrespectful toward our Heavenly Father. In response to this, my mother would wipe the tears of laughter from her eyes and remind him that even God likes to see our family laughing and playing together.

When he was around twenty years old, my father left college and went on a two year mission for his church. The most important story he tells from those years does not, at first glance, seem to have any spiritual component but it would shape the rest of his and then my own life.

He said he respected the leader of his mission because, even though he was twice my father's age, he could play basketball better than the young guns (including my dad). From this experience, my father learned that credibility is established through physical prowess. To my father, exercise was not simply a physical act; it was a form of social communication. Humans follow physically strong leaders. After his mission and college, my dad put this to use throughout his life as an Army officer by physically outcompeting his military subordinates. When he was a battalion commander, and himself twice the age of the young hotshots in his military unit, my father published his own physical fitness test scores as the standard that was expected of everyone in the unit. His score was a perfect one hundred percent. He found that when he maxed his physical fitness test it gave him credibility and earned the respect of his troops, peers, and bosses.

As a consequence of this belief, he coined another axiom: "when there is a piano to be moved, don't reach for the bench." My father joined the military at the end of the long and unpopular Vietnam War because it was the hardest thing that needed doing. He was not drafted, he volunteered. When he looked for jobs in the military he volunteered for the most difficult one he could find: Infantry. Within the Infantry he volunteered for the hardest training he could find: Ranger School. When he went to Ranger School, he found that by volunteering to carry the heaviest weapons and equipment of the platoon, he was respected. As a bonus, no one complained to him about how heavy their loads were. As they starved their way through the training, he learned that when there was food, the good leaders ensured their men ate first and they ate last if there was anything left. My dad wanted to serve in the most difficult assignments. His first assignment was to Alaska, where I was born. He dreamed of going to Antarctica.

When I look back on my father's life and the legacy and the charge he gave me, I want to ask him:

"Dad, when there were two roads, why did you always insist on taking the hard one?"

To which I imagine his reply:

"Why do you assume I see two roads?"

One of the challenges of having a father so bent on always doing the hardest things, is that it is both terrifying and exhausting to try to live up to his example, let alone the impossible challenge he had given me as a kid.

"There is no growth in the comfort zone," he'd say before setting off on another military trip with his lumpy green bags, "and no comfort in the growth zone."

"Son, you may be the only member of our family that some people ever meet. Do not embarrass our family name."

What I heard was, "Do not embarrass your father."

My father prayed every night. I remember creeping up to his room and peeking in the crack of his bedroom door one night. His back was to me, but I could see his mighty legs tucked underneath him as he knelt. His head was bowed. Through his example, he taught us to pray.

"Son, you may be the only member of our religion that some people ever meet. Do not embarrass our church. You have to live a life of superior conduct."

What I heard was, "Do not embarrass our Heavenly Father."

As a little boy I worshipped my father, and in doing so I surrendered my expectations to his. He was everything I wanted to be. He knew pretty much everything. He was tough, fast, brave, and important. He believed that no one builds self respect through pep talks. It is built by doing and mastering difficult things. It must have come from interacting with soldiers, but he worried about weakening us by making our lives too easy. My dad believed that to protect his children from the hard edges of life he had to make us strong. And the only legitimate way to do that was to set the standard of what strength looked like: to lead by example.

We camped monthly, learning to sleep on hard ground, in the snow and rain. But he also knew when to not push too hard. I remember peering out of our tent during one drenching thunderstorm and by the flashes of lightning I saw my dad out in the rain digging a ditch to divert the deluge around the tent where my younger brother and I slept. I probably still got wet, but I knew I was protected. My father was also my scoutmaster, and we went on at least one week-long campout each summer. By the time I left home after high school, I had spent more than a year of my life camping.

My father expected us to be in sports year round, and so he signed up to coach. He read daily, and expected us to read, even paying us a dollar for each book read. When I was five, he bought us bicycles and taught us how to ride by running alongside us with his longest belt wrapped around our chest so he could hold us up if we fell. Eventually he bought himself a bicycle with stirrup pedals that he rode to work each day.

When I was six years old the Army moved us to Illesheim, Germany. We lived in a small German village about seven miles from the Army post, and on Saturdays my dad would run to the post. As older kids some of us were allowed to ride along on our bicycles on these runs. I remember pedaling hard just trying to keep up with his smooth gait. Another of his axioms was, "If you don't play with your wife and kids, someone else will." Running and riding were some of his versions of play.

This was also one of the ways that my father trained for marathons. I didn't understand what these races were, or what they meant to him. All I knew was they were long, they made my mother nervous, and that even my dad considered them hard. After one marathon my older sister whispered to me about seeing our dad cross the finish line with a crazed and hurt expression in his eyes: "And then, he climbed into that fountain at the park, and he lay down in the middle of it, and I thought he was going to die."

"Nuh uh, not dad," I said, not sure if she was making this story up just to scare me.

There were eight of us kids at this time. Amongst the older ones we whispered and worried about the possibility of something ever happening to our dad… well it was a good thing we knew how to sleep in tents and cook over fires. Seeing him completely hollowed out after a marathon was one of the only times we ever sensed he might actually be mortal. Sometimes we teased him if he was walking stiffly after a difficult training session. "When you are my age, I expect you to be able to do this. This is the standard," he replied.

My father followed the ancient law, the fourth commandment: keep the Sabbath day holy. My father exercised every day except Sunday, which was the day of rest. Giving up games, exercise, and potential races on Sunday was how he interpreted the fourth commandment to keep the Sabbath day holy, it was part of how he worshipped God. He agreed with the movie <u>Chariots of Fire</u>: don't run on the Sabbath. Like the movie's hero, Eric Liddell, my father believed, "God made me, but He also made me fast; and I can feel His pleasure when I run." On Sunday he sometimes allowed himself to take an afternoon nap. Or was it that on Sunday he had *earned* his afternoon nap?

When I was a teenager, the route of our city's marathon ran down the street in front of our church. My father seemed haunted each year that he was not able to run in it perhaps because other military men from our congregation ran in it. Though my mom teased him about his moodiness on those days, I understood that not running was difficult for him.

One day, he told me about a new race, something called the Ironman, where people swam 2.4 miles, then rode their bikes over a hundred miles, and *then* ran a marathon. The race was 140.6 miles long. Like many Americans, my dad had watched Julie Moss crawl her way across the finish line at Kona, Hawaii. He was filled with the level of awe that borders on horror. He said it was crazy, but over the years he started following it as a sport. He even started doing triathlons, frequently riding his aging bike to the race course to serve notice to the other competitors, and then riding it home afterward.

When his races were over my dad would call us together as a family and reveal the race t-shirt he had earned. He didn't keep them for himself; he took turns giving them to us kids to use as pajama shirts. Though he didn't say it, I often felt like those shirts were magic. They couldn't be bought in stores. Those shirts could only be earned by running really fast, and so I believed that if I slept in mine, I would run faster the next day.

Like any son, I wanted desperately to make my father proud. I knew his own parents were proud of him—their only son, their son the college graduate, their son the Army officer. I knew this because their letters addressed my father by his military rank. My mom teased him about this family formality. But I knew how formal his parents were. I read between the lines: they were proud of him.

My dad worked hard, doing important things, and we learned not to bother him too much, unless it was something important. When he took battalion command my mother told me that she felt like my dad was driving a huge ship, and she was just a little dinghy that was tied to him by a long rope, dragging along behind him. That was how I felt too, pumping my little bike pedals furiously and watching him as he ran smoothly, lost in his grownup thoughts.

I wanted to live up to his standards, to honor him and show him that I was listening, and that I had heard what he had spent my lifetime trying to teach me.

But part of me was afraid.

Part of me is always afraid.

I was afraid that if I were to actually live up to the charge he had given me when I was four, I would be competing with the ghost of his legacy. I knew how fast he could run. I knew how far he could run. I knew how deeply his disappointment could hurt when I didn't measure up. But I was even more afraid of surpassing him. I was afraid that if I actually lived up to my father's expectation and became a better man, then it would offend him. Or, worse yet, it would diminish him from this god-like figure down to human proportions. And I needed my dad to be larger than life because life was so much larger than me.

Like my father and mother before me, after a year of college, I too left to serve as a missionary for two years. I was devoting a tithe of ten percent of my twenty year life serving God. So, I was teaching in the Amazon region of Brazil when I received a letter (labeled with my religious title) from my dad telling me that he was writing to me from a hospital bed.

With his strangely angular handwriting, he wrote that he had had an accident while playing volleyball with his troops. As he had done countless times over his years in the military, he had jumped to crush a spike on one of his students to show them who was boss. But this time, when his mighty quadricep had fired to launch him into the air, it ripped the patellar tendon right off its anchors on his shin, reeled his kneecap up into his thigh, and sent him crashing onto the floor in uncontrollable spasms of pain. He wrote that he had just had surgery to reattach it.

And so, in the months I spent teaching people about an all-loving and all-powerful Heavenly Father, my father limped around in a cast with his crutches.

My mother later told me that the day he got his cast off he went to the swimming pool and swam and swam, trying to reclaim his strength. Fitness was too deep a part of his identity for him to stop just because he had ripped one of his kneecaps off.

"Better to wear out than to rust out," he said as he set about finding new ways to wear himself out.

He continued to go to sleep early, to get up early to pray and then to exercise. He continued swimming and added in more bicycling.

When I returned from my mission he gave me a bicycle and told me I was going with his Boy Scout troop on a bike trip. We rode across Nebraska and Wyoming to Utah to reenact a pioneer trek. We averaged seventy to a hundred miles a day, my father still pedaling his fifteen-year-old bike. "Tired Scouts are easy to lead," he said at the end of each day's ride. He ensured they had enough to eat. Then he ate last. The scouts grew in self-confidence from doing hard things, and also in their confidence of his leadership.

However, he became cautious about running. For years thereafter, my dad spoke of the ache in his "rebuilt" knee. Like the invulnerable Achilles, my father's weakness proved to be a tendon. Strangely, that weakness gave me a path out of the paradox I was trapped in. On the one hand, my father had charged me with living up to (and exceeding?) his example. But on the other hand, I did not wish to challenge or in any way to tarnish his legacy. If he was hurt, then it was not really his fault that he could not run like the tireless wolf he had once been. And it was not really my fault if I could run faster than him. His injury gave me a guilty self-confidence. At the same time I wanted to help rebuild my father's confidence. I wanted to trick him back onto the pedestal of invulnerability from which he had fallen and that I needed him to reoccupy.

Feeling like I was still just a little boy, I wanted to put my hands on his shoulders and tell him that he couldn't get hurt anymore. I needed him to be better.

We, who like the Happy Warrior, are doomed
to go in company with pain and fear and bloodshed
have a higher mission than other men,
and it is for us to see that we are not unworthy.
Berkeley Moynihan, Surgeon

If you haven't felt like quitting,
your dreams aren't big enough.
Anonymous

MILE 2
The Run Less Traveled

Atelphobia: (Greek) (n) the fear of not being good enough.

One morning of my senior year of high school, Dr. Groo—a pathologist who attended my church—called and asked me if I would like to skip school to do something educational instead.

"What?" I asked. A doctor encouraging me to skip school was exhilarating. I had no idea that real education could change the course of my life.

"Last night a man was killed, and we are doing an autopsy this morning to figure out why he died. Come on down, this'll be interesting."

Another friend and I went down to the blue-tiled morgue. The man's body lay unmoving and dead on a cold stainless steel table. He had the kind of stillness that made me hold my breath.

Against his unapologetic nakedness we were given special clothes, masks and aprons. The pathologist and his assistants made a few preliminary observations of the outside of the man's body, noting various injuries and the locations of bruises and bloodstains that meant nothing to me. Then, they got out a scalpel, stuck it into the base of the man's neck and used it to draw a straight, bloodless line to his groin. When they opened his abdomen, I peered into a virgin world that was completely uncharted and unknown to me. I blinked repeatedly, trying to make sense of the unfamiliar shapes and smells of death. I was surprised at the colors in what had always been blank dark areas of myself. The pathologist preceded onward undaunted, plucking alien-appearing specimens from the damp chaos and then creating order by pronouncing their strange names aloud, weighing them, and describing other findings to his scribing assistants. I was given a clipboard and told how to spell the names and findings as we continued. The stems of a thick dark organ were clipped and it was plucked out of the man with two hands. The spacey, curvy organ was proclaimed his liver, and the locations and lengths of the lacerations on its surface were noted. The specimens were placed into an orderly array of smartly labeled buckets, bowls, and basins; lids were snapped crisply into place. Strange tools appeared, jaws clamping just so, hungry needles buried themselves up to their hubs and suddenly they were full of bile, or blood, or vitreous that went into more neat containers for further study at "the lab" later. Bone saws screamed through obstructing ribs into his chest and then skull as we continued to chart and to map our way through the man's organs and injuries.

That autopsy was the single most educational experience I ever had in high school. When I finally went home, my mind was burning with exhilaration over what we had just done. From that man's death, a new crazy idea was born: I wanted to go to medical school! My favorite uncle, my uncle Gilbert, was a family physician. I loved and respected him, but until that day I never knew I could be like him.

Up to that point in my life, I had wanted to be a writer. By paying us a dollar for every book we read, my parents had shaped my life and love of books. Well-crafted sentences, perfect descriptions and sound syllogisms that blew my mind were proof that humans could do magic. A writer's choice of words could make the familiar new, and the new familiar. I wanted to feel awe and wonder. I wanted to create weave entire worlds into existence with my own magic words.

David McCullough wrote, "Writing is thinking. To write well is to think clearly. That is why it is so hard." I wanted to think clearly. I wanted to think hard. I wanted to think with great precision.

"The act of putting pen to paper encourages pause for thought, this in turn makes us think more deeply about life, which helps us regain our equilibrium," wrote Norbet Platt. I wanted to regain my equilibrium! Writers paid attention to the world around them and the words inside of them. I wanted to pay attention. But most of all, I wanted to feel things deeply and to feel like my life made a difference. I wanted to write words that kindled the pages they were written on to light minds on fire.

"Dad, have you ever wanted to write a book?"

"Oh son, I love reading, but writing is not for everyone."

I told my father that I couldn't decide between being a writer or a doctor. He thought for a moment.

"You can always be a doctor who writes, but you cannot be a writer who doctors," he said. In other words: there aren't really two roads. There is only one road: delay gratification. Choosing the harder option first preserves the other options.

Inside myself there was something that felt relieved. Being a writer was not self-abnegating enough. Secretly, I thought that being a writer seemed too self-indulgent, too awesome, and too special. Who was I to think *I* could do that?

Later, when I told my mission and college friends that I dreamed of going to medical school, they said it would take too long, or be too hard. I thought about that concern, and then dismissed it. The grueling duration of medical school was the very source of its glory. After all, my father's lesson and legacy to me was that I was the heir of a marathoner, not a sprinter.

As I studied in undergrad to prepare for medical school, I made a promise to God one night as I said my prayers. I said, "Dear God, if you help me get in to medical school and become a doctor, I promise that I will devote all that I learn to serve you."

When I interviewed to get in to medical school, I was asked what I wanted to study. I told them of the images I had seen of children starving in the famine in Ethiopia. I frowned earnestly and told him that I wasn't sure, but that I wanted to help combat childhood starvation.

The interviewer smiled and made a note on my application.

When my wife Katie and I completed our undergraduate studies at the University of Kansas, each of the various schools stood to cheer at the commencement. When the students who were graduating from the medical school stood, cheered, and sprayed each other with celebratory bottles of champagne, one of the students near us in the business school shook his head and said, "They deserve it, they've been through hell."

My wife Katie looked at me, eyebrows raised questioningly. I grinned back at her: I couldn't wait to go!

During undergrad, I worked at UPS to put myself and my wife through college. It felt good to move after studying all day, and then it felt good to sit down in the lecture halls after moving all night. Once I got to medical school, I only exercised occasionally. The material was fascinating, but it came so fast that it was difficult to find enough time to study and listen to the lectures. I learned of the innumerous ways the human body could malfunction: drinking too much water could dilute the salts in the blood to levels so low hyponatremia could kill you. Exercise too much too fast and muscles break down, release their contents and potentially lead to kidney failure. Infections could attack the body: staph, herpes, meningitis, etcetera. The body could attack itself: hypothyroidism, rheumatoid arthritis, and cancers. The mind could attack the body with distorted beliefs and delusions leading to anxiety and depressions so deep that people held themselves hostage in suicidal gestures and acts.

I gained thirty pounds as I sat and studied diabetes, hypertension and the obesity epidemic in our country. I struggled to fit all the material into my brain. I bought bigger pants. Some tests were worse than others. After leading most of my classes throughout undergrad, I found myself squarely in the middle of my medical school class. I didn't know how the other students did so well. The classmates who surrounded me worked harder than anyone I had ever met. On top of excellent grades, many of them were doing triathlons, or running marathons.

Meanwhile, I gained weight, and my hair continued to fall out. Self-consciousness sprouted in the vacant space it left behind. Self-doubts began to eat at me as I ate another bagel and read another page and took another test. As they gnawed at me, I tried to soothe my anxious mind, and stay awake, by snacking. When I didn't do well on a test my self-doubts grew and organized and began whispering to me.

Going into medical school, I didn't know exactly what kind of a doctor I wanted to be. Though Dr. Groo had started my interest with pathology, I loved our parasitology and microbiology classes. The tactics of germs and parasites and weapons of antibiotics and other antimicrobial medicines all seemed like a video game, so I pictured myself going into internal medicine and then sub-specializing in infectious diseases. Then, after two years of constant studying and testing, I finally got to go to the hospitals and actually see patients!

My first clinical rotation was in family medicine. The junior doctors—called resident physicians—were delivering babies, admitting patients from the emergency room, doing their rounds on sick in-patients and seeing a breathtaking variety of problems in their clinics. In short, they were doing what I had always thought was what doctors did. These were real doctors, and I wanted to be like them. Every rotation after that, with every subsequent specialty made me think, "Hey, this is also cool, and I can still do this in family medicine!" Pediatrics, Obstetrics, Internal Medicine: yes, yes, yes! I could see why my uncle Gilbert had chosen family medicine, and I wanted to be like him.

At the beginning of the fourth year of medical school, the fall rotations are selected so students can interview with residency programs where they would like to receive specialty training. And so, as my third year drew to a close, I submitted my schedule request to rotate and interview at family medicine programs.

And then, just before heading off to interview, I arrived at my final rotation of my third year of medical school: General Surgery. I had no concept of what surgery was like except for what I had seen in television or movies. After covering our heads, masking our faces, and washing ceremoniously with lovely iodine-smelling soap, we entered the secret rooms of the hospital: the surgical suite. There we were carefully dressed in sterile robes, gloved, and transformed. The tools, drawers and magnifiers reminded me of my grandfather's work shop. Only it was much brighter, and had a warm, breathing human body on the work bench. Just as I had experienced with Dr. Groo, there was a slightly sickening feeling of sticking a knife into someone's body, but this time it was alive and it bled. Then a world was peeled open that few people ever see. It was the only time in all of medical school I felt the exhilaration I had felt while watching the autopsy back in high school. The hairs on my arms stood up, my mouth went dry, and my ears began to buzz as I was handed the medical student's tool: the retractor.

Holding skin, or muscles, or other organs out of the way for them, the surgeons and their surgical residents excavated into human bodies as a deft, focused team in what they called surgical *explorations*, returning with slime-faced tumors, bloated and weeping gallbladders, or taut angry appendixes that were plopped defenseless into jars of formaldehyde. I imagined their angry faces pressed against the jars, screaming silent streams of bubbles at us. Teratomas, tumors filled with jumbled pieces of life—hair, teeth, and bones—but none of life's elegant organization, were exorcised. Diseases were neatly separated from the patients. Then, the tracks of our invasion were covered with quick smooth throws of curved needles. The retractor shifted up, layers were closed, and the team retreated.

Now that, I could not do in family medicine!

I had already set up my fourth year rotations to interview at family medicine residencies, but now I wanted to switch to surgery. I had to switch, I felt it!

And that was when the voices of my self-doubts, fully trained and articulately developed, cleared their throats behind me.

"Who do you think you are to do surgery?"

"Please don't," I said.

I could hear them smile sticky smiles at each other. Without looking I knew their basement-colored eyes were staring at me.

"Surgery is five years long; you're already older than most people here because you took time off of college to be a missionary. Don't you know you're too old?"

"Leave me alone," I said, trying to sound confident.

"What about those questions you missed back in anatomy class? If you don't know everything perfectly, you'll kill someone!"

"I can study. I can learn."

"Surgery is the most difficult residency. You can't handle that, you're just barely handling medical school."

"I can handle it," I said.

"Surgery is for the top students in their class, and you are in the middle of yours. What are you trying to do, kill someone with your mediocrity?"

"I can try to catch up," I said, "Besides, most of the top students don't even want to keep doing something difficult, they want to use their hard work to get into the easy specialties like dermatology, or ophthalmology."

"People in surgery are confident and aggressive; you aren't either of those things or we wouldn't even be here. Why don't you find a specialty that fits your personality, like family medicine?"

"But the personality tests in college told me not to even go into medicine! They said I should be a flight attendant! I don't believe in them. Besides, I've met nice surgeons. Why can't I be a nice surgeon?"

"People who go into surgery all have family members who are surgeons. They've already taught them the tips and tricks necessary to excel. No one in your family is a surgeon. You're even further behind."

"But I could be the first; I could set a new standard for what is possible for my family!"

"Surgery has crazy hours. What are you trying to do? You want to abandon your wife and kids? You'll end up divorced!"

"Hey, if you don't play with your wife and kids, someone else will!" the other voice said.

"My wife said she'll support me."

"She doesn't even know what she's committing to!" the voices laughed.

"She didn't completely know what she was committing to when she married me either, but she still did it."

"And, um, how's that working out for her?"

"Don't talk about her."

The chamber of my mind echoed the sound of my self-doubts through their amplifying acoustics. Just like being a writer, surgery felt like it would be too hard to get into, and too hard to complete. At the same time, it seemed *too* fun, and *too* fascinating, *too* incredible for a normal someone like me. In the words of Scott Lynch, "I was afflicted by two simultaneous yet contradictory delusions—the burning certainty that I was a unique genius destined for greatness and the constant fear that I was a witless fraud speeding toward epic failure."

I made an effort at changing my rotations, but was met with too much resistance. I was told changing them so late in the year was like trying to turn a battleship on a dime. It was too late.

Once again I felt like a little boy being told that I could not follow the thing I felt called to do. I didn't understand. I could feel my bones straining for the weight of the adventure I was supposed to have stacked on my shoulders. I was supposed to choose the harder path. But sometimes the road less traveled is closed for a season, or overgrown with obstacles and doubts. I repeated my promise to myself: I will prepare, and someday…

I accepted the love and the life I believed I deserved. I made my peace. I went into family medicine.

We either make ourselves miserable
or we make ourselves strong.
The amount of work is the same.
Carlos Castaneda, Anthropologist

Unless you learn to face your own shadows,
you will continue to see them in others, because the world outside
of you is only a reflection of the world inside of you.
Anonymous

MILE 3
The Pain Container

Ibrat: (Urdu) (n) an anguish arising out of the suffering of others.

Because I had attended the military's medical school, I was accepted to a military family medicine residency. When I arrived, along with my seven classmates who had attended civilian medical schools, we were given a physical fitness test. I looked at my classmates and smiled to myself. Some of them admitted that they hadn't exercised for the entire four years of medical school. One of them was far chubbier than I had become. As my father had taught me, I would establish credibility through physical prowess. The night before, I told my wife that I planned to beat everyone. I wanted to use fitness to serve notice of who I was.

I came in fourth place out of eight.

I had served notice alright: to myself.

Most shocking to me was that the classmate who won was both shorter than me, and slightly chubby. When I wheezed my way across the finish line, I couldn't believe what had happened. I had been a runner in high school. I knew I could run faster than that. But after a two-year mission, four years of college, and four years of medical school, I had lost touch with some of the people I used to be.

Evaluating the evidence, my self-doubts started laughing at my identity confusion.

"That extra thirty pounds looked heavy."

"If you are a runner," the doubts said, elbowing each other, "then what the heck was that?"

"Welcome to the new you."

These thoughts soaked me in sadness until they blocked out all sound. This was not the me I wanted to be.

I knew my dad would ask about how I did. I was embarrassed. In that moment of discouragement, when I was not sure if I could believe in myself I found a way to quiet the voices: I drew strength from my father's legacy. When he was my age, he was running marathons. No one laughed at his speed or at his endurance. I was his son. The blood of a marathoner flowed in my veins, dormant and diluted perhaps, but undeniable. I drew strength from the fact that though it had been a long time, I had once been a runner. I had once been faster than that performance. Within me beat the heart of a better man. I needed to meet some of the people I wanted to become.

In the midst of the disconnect I felt between what I believed and what I had actually achieved, I turned to one of the tools that my parents had taught me to love: books. M. Scott Peck had written about the "healthiness of depression." He wrote that depression can be healthy because it can create sorrow of sufficient intensity to create change even when we don't want to.

In the following days of embarrassed discouragement I made a vow. If my life was my story, then I decided that this was not how my story was going to go. This was not the me I wanted to be. I vowed I would follow my father's example and get a one hundred percent on the next PT test. But I knew my track record with setting resolutions and then not following through. I needed more than an internal, self-imposed vow. I needed a powerful external force to hold me accountable for achieving my own dream.

I needed peer pressure.

So, modeled after my father's stories, and on behalf of my fellow residents, I challenged the faculty physicians to a competition based on our next PT test scores. Once I had thrown the gauntlet down, I was committed. I began exercising again. Slowly the pounds came off my body and the seconds came off my run time. Slowly I became stronger. Slowly I became faster.

I started doing push-ups and sit-ups every evening. A deadline was approaching.

I noticed that when I ran, my thoughts narrowed. Instead of the countless wavering worries that swirled about me when I sat or walked, when I ran I could only hold one thought at a time. When the time came for me to test again, I auditioned and then consciously chose that one thought. As the pain in my legs and lungs increased I repeated it to myself over and over with each racing step:

"I can take more pain than this."

"I can take more pain than this."

"I can take more pain than this."

Other thoughts tried to push their way in, especially as the burn increased and worries waved that I could not keep this up. I pushed them out of my mind and repeated my mantra. I believed it.

When I crossed the finish line, I felt my stomach rise threateningly, but it settled as I struggled to breathe.

I had scored a perfect one hundred percent.

From that victory, a little seed of self-confidence was planted. This was the me I was supposed to be. This was me living up to the standard.

Then, just as I was improving in one area, other areas of my life started caving in.

Residency was like falling down a long hole. I arrived at the hospital before the sun. It was a weird and fantastical world, illuminated by the bluish sunlight of fluorescent lights, that didn't make sense. When I left it was dark again. People entered the strange world and were transformed. Names were lost, replaced with diagnostic labels. Clothes were exchanged for gowns. Names were replaced with diagnoses "the liver in room 214."

Even words were traded until an entire new language was spoken. "Walking," became "ambulating." "Red," transmuted into "erythema." People no longer "ate," instead they "fed."

My anxious, worrying mind mixed with the anxious worrying minds of my patients. I hurt with them, and their hurt was breathtaking. I struggled with knowing how to set boundaries. Which of their choices was I responsible for? I believed that if one of my patients smoked, it was because *I* had not been a good enough doctor. I hadn't studied "motivational interviewing" well enough. If one of my patients got a new diagnosis of diabetes, it was because *I* hadn't done a good enough job teaching them to eat well. When I was at the hospital, when a sick patient went into cardiac arrest, it was because *I* had missed something. When my sister's son died, I blamed myself because *I* wasn't able to be there to protect him and to help her.

I felt like I was suffocating under the collective weight of the patients' sick, swollen bodies and distended medical charts. There were so many overweight people. There were so many patients with high blood pressure, and high cholesterol. There was so much diabetes. So many patients came to the hospital with chest pain and cancer. Obese pregnant women who had never exercised quit in the middle of pushing their children into life and begged for cesarean sections instead. And so their children were born by the strength and skill of someone other than their own mother.

Despite our efforts to keep them alive, some patients were bent on hurting themselves. Depressed people got to be both the hostage of their sorrows and the hostage-taker with undefined demands; both the victim and the perpetrator. As I sewed up one young woman's slit wrists I wondered why. Her depression both fascinated and repulsed me. It was both completely alien and completely familiar.

I listened to an endless train of pain roll by. People with their various complaints and problems flashed briefly through my appointment room on their way to their destinations. Back pain, abdominal pain, knee pain, chest pain. Droves of faceless people flew by with raised hands begging me to give them "something for the pain." I tried to focus on the passing, flashing faces to recognize at least one as the train went by. I tried to recognize if any of the flashing faces belonged to immediately dangerous diseases, and worried constantly that I had missed one.

Things felt upside down. I thought practicing medicine would be about helping people get healthier. Yet, many times I began to feel that some medications seemed marketed to patients, not to make them healthy, but to sell them on the possibility that they were sick. These medicines were marketed to doctors by slick "drug reps" who bought us lunch and fed our desire to be treated special because we were doctors. We ate first. If there was anything left, the nurses and technicians were allowed to have the scraps.

Many times, I felt like a marriage counselor. Patients came in because their minds and their bodies were arguing. They wanted me to take sides.

"Tell my body to stop getting diabetes just because I drink two liters of soda a day."

"Hey, can you give me a pill to lose weight so I don't have to change anything?"

"Isn't there some medicine I can take that will allow me to keep eating like this without getting high cholesterol?"

"Doc, can you just give me something for my lungs so I don't have to quit smoking?"

"Doc, can you just give me a CPAP machine for my sleep apnea so I don't have to lose weight?"

I wanted to tell them, "Look, I know it's hard to quit smoking, but it's also hard to have lung cancer! Yes it is hard to eat healthy, but it is also hard being overweight. It is hard to exercise every day, but it is also going to be hard when your high blood pressure causes a stroke. Since it's going to be hard either way, just choose the right hard!"

I grimly began to understand why, back when I was trying to get into medical school, the interviewer had smiled when I had said I wanted to help combat childhood starvation: because in America, many the health problems were caused by the exact opposite of starvation.

I tried to be helpful, I thought that maybe I could absorb their pain. I learned that the word "compassion" came from two Latin root words, "com" meaning "with," and "passion," meaning "to feel." In exercising compassion for my patients, I felt their pains, their fears, and their diseases with them. In doing so, I discovered that it isn't just infections that are contagious, so was pain. Andrew Boyd put it like this, "Compassion hurts. When you feel connected to everything you also feel responsible for everything. And you cannot turn away. Your destiny is bound with the destinies of others. You must either learn to carry the Universe or be crushed by it. You must grow strong enough to love the world, yet empty enough to sit down at the same table with its worst horrors."

When you physically touch another person, you can actually alter the chemistry of their body. Oxytocin is released when hugging another human, or when petting a dog. But I was discovering that touching another person's problems and worries was also changing me. Rose McDermott from Brown University and her colleagues published a study in 2009 that found that when you have friends that divorce, it increases your own chances of getting a divorce by seventy-five percent. I wondered if there were similar odds if a friend gains weight, has a heart attack, or gets cancer.

When I went home, seeing my wife and kids was like peering through a periscope at the world as it was on the real surface, before I fell into this place. They went to school and to parks; my wife went shopping, and talked on the phone with her mother and sister. The normality of their lives was like a life boat that didn't know had been built for a storm.

It started to be too much. As the train sped past, melting into a single fluid movement, it began to pull me off the station and into its current. I didn't realize I was drowning because I was trying so hard to be everyone else's anchor. The pain began overflowing not just into my personal life, but into my dreams.

I remember one specific nightmare that I had during residency. In the dream, the world was in a post-apocalyptic decay. I was working at the hospital, and the patients would come in and their bodies would fall apart into little white dice. Using our gloved hands, my fellow residents and I would try to push the little cubes back into the shape of a human body. The other doctors began eating hospital food, wearing hospital clothes, dating and marrying each other. They never left the hospital. I told them I needed to leave, I had to get to my family—my wife, son and little daughter. They all laughed.

I went outside, and there was a fire truck spraying the decayed and burning houses. But then I saw that the water tank was actually stamped, "Gasoline." It had been painted over.

I ran to our house, ahead of the gasoline-spraying fire truck. The screen door hung crooked on the hinges.

I went in. My young daughter was standing there with skinny legs and a swollen abdomen, like the starving children with kwashiorkor from my medical textbooks. She was trying to feed herself, eating candy with decaying teeth. I asked where her mom was, and she pointed to the bedroom. I went in. My wife was lying in bed sick. I told her to get up, that I needed her help. She sloshed back and forth in the bed, but said she could not get up anymore because she was too sick. I kicked at the bed and yelled at her to get up, that I needed her help. She couldn't get up.

I woke from that dream crying and shaking, and feeling like everyone and everything was dying and decaying.

The voices of self-doubt laughed and laughed at me. Side-splitting, tear-pouring, snot-dripping laughter.

"You know you are the only resident who is having nightmares?"

"Real doctors can hold themselves together."

In this low mental state, the sickness and suffering and dying all around me overthrew my sanity. I turned to something to try to—in the words of my narcotic-seeking patients—"shut my brain off." I fell into addiction. My mind spiraled out of control and I made some very poor decisions. Not only were my patients and my sanity dying, my marriage also started withering and decaying. My nightmare about the post-apocalyptic world was coming true.

One night I had an addiction dream. There was a police officer walking a white German Shepherd. Loving dogs, I reached down to pet it. Its jaws clamped down on my hand. It stared up at me with fierce eyes, not letting go. Pain shot up my arm. I started panicking and praying for help.

The policeman reached down and touched it. It let go.

I rubbed my throbbing hand, but wanted to show the dog that I didn't have any hard feelings, and hoping we could be friends. So I reached down once more to pet it, and once again it bit me. Despite the blinding pain I tried to be calm, to touch it like the police officer had, but it just squeezed its jaws tighter. I started to panic once again when I realized I couldn't get it to let go. The police officer came by and asked me if I would like the dog to let go, and I said, "Yes." He touched it again, and again it went soft and let go.

Then I saw two little ducklings walking through the backdoor into the backyard. One was a little boy duckling and the other was a little girl duckling. I looked and the white dog had seen them too. It was staring at them, and standing up. A little Asian sparrow flew down to walk with the ducklings. It was about the same size as them, even though it was full-grown. None of them had seen the destructive danger of this white dog. I saw the dog's muscles tense as it prepared to jump at all three of them. I grabbed it. The dog twisted in my grip, snapping at me and wrapping its body around me. It squirmed inside of my shirt and I could feel its claws on my ribs and back. Its jaws were snapping at me, but it didn't have enough room to move under the shirt to bite me. It also couldn't get to the little birds, but it was hurting me as it writhed under my shirt, inside my own skin looking for my neck.

I looked for the police officer, but couldn't see in my blinded panic. I cried out, "Officer! Help me!"

I woke up crying again.

During residency, as the chaos of diseases and people's unhealthy choices overwhelmed me, my wife left me twice, taking our two kids with her. Somehow she knew to draw a line around me, a boundary, so that the infectious hurt that haunted me did not spread to her. And she would protect our kids from me if she had to.

I told my church leader what was happening, I was released from my church responsibilities, and told I could no longer pray in meetings.

"I feel like you are kicking me out of a hospital for being sick."

"No, you're getting kicked out for choosing to be sick."

"You think I chose this? I can't control it anymore."

"Then go to addiction recovery."

I struggled in my relationship with God, that great Police Officer who enforced eternal laws. One large series of problems arose from people's poor choices and habits, but a second set seemed to come from just arbitrary bad luck: cancer, autoimmune diseases, car crashes, and infections. Even chaos has a pattern, and if anyone can influence these types of problems, it had to be Heavenly Father. But He seemed so far away, so busy. I knelt down and prayed each night as my parents had taught me. But many nights, when I prayed, I could no longer tell if He was there, or if I was just talking to myself. I asked Heavenly Father where He was, and why He was allowing all of this to happen. Why wasn't He helping these people? Why wasn't He helping me?

"You asked for my help to get into medical school."

"Yeah, well, you should have known it would be like this. You should have known better than me."

"I do. That is what 'omniscient' means."

"If you are there, then why is there so much disease in the world? Why is there so much suffering? Why don't you do something?"

"Why do you believe I don't?"

"Because they got worse! And that beautiful little girl started seizing and stopped breathing and I needed your help. *She* needed your help! I needed your help when that lady was coding in the ER. The whole family was looking at me, and the nurses, and she died."

"I know."

"I don't believe in you anymore."

"It's okay to be angry. I'm strong enough I can take it."

"Yeah, well I'm not strong enough to take it."

"Do you believe I can make you stronger?"

"I'm not talking to you anymore."

No one was taking good care of their bodies. Everyone was smoking and eating themselves to death. It was horrible to watch people drowning each day, and not being able to convince them that they could save themselves by just standing up. My wife and church leaders probably felt the same way about me.

I needed a way to stop letting people pull me into their storms. I needed a way to pull myself (and then maybe my patients) out of their storms and into a more peaceful place. I needed some way to push back against all the sickness and disease that engulfed me. I needed some way to win back my wife's heart, to impress her and to regain her admiration. I wanted my patients to learn how to suffer better, and I wanted to learn how to suffer better myself. Maybe it wasn't the patients who were sick, maybe it was me. I needed a way to run for my life. If pain was contagious, was strength?

In my study of addiction recovery, I came across the a quote by Patrick Carnes that hit me like an arrow deep into my heart, vibrating with truth: "Loving and nurturing our bodies is a metaphor for every spiritual task we face and is our primary spiritual responsibility. It precedes and symbolizes all other responsibilities...physical exercise is an essentially spiritual discipline that we must practice until we die. In the West, we tend to see fitness as an optional health concern that can be a low priority in a busy schedule. We make physical fitness into a competition and confer status symbols—Olympic gold medals or multi-million-dollar contracts—on a few gifted athletes. Occasionally, when someone refers to the runner's high, or the 'Zen' of weightlifting, we glimpse the more profound connection between mind and body. When we separate these positive experiences from the rest of life, we split the two and add to our spiritual damage."

Having a front row seat on this circus of anti-athleticism, I could see that this separation also added to my patients' physical damage. It had certainly added to my own mental damage.

Exploring Edges

All parents damage their children.
Mitch Albom, Writer

Life breaks us all,
but some of us grow stronger in the broken areas.
Earnest Hemmingway, Writer

MILE 4
The Rescue: Operation Priceless

Kintsukuroi: (Japanese) (n) "to repair with gold"; the art of repairing broken pottery with gold or silver and understanding that the piece is more beautiful for having been broken.

In the midst of the storm of suffering that my life had become, I thought about the one area of my life where I was experiencing some success: fitness. After two and a half years of saying the same things over and over about exercise to patients I started to wonder if life was telling me to say it over and over until I finally heard and believed it myself. Maybe I wasn't supposed to be an anchor for them. Maybe I was supposed to be a lighthouse. Anne Lamott once said, "Lighthouses don't go running all over an island looking for boats to save; they just stand there shining." Maybe if I was going to help my patients I had to lead by example. As Mahatma Gandhi had taught, "be the change you wish to see in the world." I wanted the world to exercise. Thich Nhat Hanh once said, "When you learn how to suffer, you suffer much less." A crazy idea germinated in my mind.

Ten years after my father's knee injury, I told him that I was thinking about running a marathon before graduating from residency. None of my other seven siblings had claimed this part of his legacy. My father's voice quickened when I told him my idea. He began giving me tips from back when he ran marathons. I sensed an opening.

I asked him if he would run it with me.

There was a little pause in the conversation. Or maybe it was just me holding my breath. In that silence I could feel him weighing the potential adventure against the caution he now felt with his knee. I needed his help to tackle this thing called a marathon and I could feel time ticking away from both of us. I was thirty-two and my father was fifty-eight. I needed his help because I did not know if I could run it on my own. The territory was too foreign, too savage, too intimidating. I needed a guide. I had learned that sometimes I needed other people's help to achieve my dreams. Also, I desperately wanted him to be proud of me. I needed someone to admire me.

I don't know what he was thinking during that pause, but I imagined he was remembering the charge he had given me years ago, and sensed I was still working at it. I imagined him sensing the vulnerability of his son. Finally he let out a slow breath and said, "Yeah, I think I could run one more. I think I have at least one more marathon left in me." Like sound of a familiar engine turning over, I could hear his enthusiasm warming and then revving up as we spoke.

Like two explorers planning an expedition, we began spending our Sunday evening phone calls talking about our training plans, how his knee was doing, running shoes, and what kinds of miles we were up to. I felt like I was being given access to his secret papers and vaults of knowledge on the subject. I had asked and was willing to train, so he was willing to pass his hard-earned knowledge on to me.

To ease the pain of the increasing mileage on his knee, my dad told me that he had finally allowed himself to buy a new bike. He owned his last one for twenty-six years. He gave me the stirrup pedals.

As we looked for a marathon, we had two rules: first, it had to be within driving distance. Second, it could not be on a Sunday. Though running with me was important, my father's obedience to his God was even more so.

Listening to the voices of self-doubt that told me I was no longer a runner, I bought a book called *The Non-Runner's Marathon Trainer.* The authors, David Whitsett and Forrest A. Dolgener, actually developed and taught a college course at the University of Northern Iowa in which their students would increase their running distances over the course of a semester and run a full marathon as their final. In the years of teaching this course, they had experimented with different training regimens and amassed enormous experience.

There were three items in the book that were pivotal.

First, there was a chart showing that it is possible to train for a marathon by running only four days a week. That was critical because I was working sixty to eighty hours a week in residency. The chart showed how to gradually increase the miles run each week. Each week-end needed a "long run" that became progressively longer. The book warned that I would not be able to run a great distance without preparation. It hinted at an upper speed limit of human adaptation, and that if I tried to rush it, I risked breaking the speed limit and paying the speeding fine in pain or injuries. It was a relief that I did not have to rush; in fact, it was physically impossible (or at least foolish) to rush into such a big goal.

The second thing I learned from this book was to deliberately and intentionally control my mental self-talk. Our minds marinade in the flavors of our thoughts. If they are not controlled, self-doubts will preemptively kill more dreams than actual failures. I already knew that in the privacy of my own mind my self-doubts second guessed and critiqued me harshly and relentlessly. Sometimes my mind would almost scratch itself raw.

The book taught that if you run, then you are allowed to call yourself a runner. If you run a marathon, you are allowed to call yourself a marathoner. This refreshing permission countered my voices of self-doubt.

"Did I run today?"

"Yes, but not very far, or very fast…"

"The qualifiers don't matter. You are a runner."

"Really?"

"Yes, you are a runner."

"Did I support, guide, or play with my kids today?"

"Yes, but not very much, and…"

"Again, the qualifiers don't matter. You are allowed to call yourself a father."

Third, I learned that if I was going to run a marathon, then I had to be prepared for when my body would start to hurt. Pain and discomfort are unavoidable when running a marathon. But the pain can be managed. As Buddhism teaches, "pain is inevitable, suffering is optional." If I trained my body, then my mind would follow. And if I trained my mind, then my body would follow.

I started following the book's training program. But initially, like many dreams, this one proved fragile and delicate. I had to protect it, to shield it. I didn't tell many people about it because I worried that one laugh, one critical comment might cause it to collapse. I spent much of the winter running on a treadmill in my basement after my kids had gone to bed. I ran and watched Ultimate Fighting Championship. I watched warriors, and turned the treadmill all the way up for each of the final rounds to feel exhausted with them, to leave everything out there.

On Saturdays, I did my long runs outside. It was wonderful to be outside, to be under the natural light of the sun, and to feel the wind. It was wonderful to be outside running for my life and doing something to make my body better, stronger and healthier. I couldn't change the countless patients who wouldn't exercise, but I could change myself. I looked at my balding head and shaved the rest off.

One of the strange benefits of training and running was that it quieted my mind. Some people are warriors, and some people are worriers. As a member of the latter class, I found that running gave me something legitimate to worry my mind with. It gave my worries a bone to chew on. It provided order and repetition to wear them down. And when they flared up anyway, I could plan in advance how I would discipline them. My worries and self-doubts didn't have time to speak because I was too busy just trying to keep breathing. My addictive cravings decreased as I threw myself into the training. I learned that much of addiction comes from turning to something to drown out the voices of self-doubt in our minds. Exercise did that for me. It helped my mind to quiet. I learned that self-doubts and worries, for all their tenacity, are not particularly strong runners.

When the day of the marathon finally arrived, my wife did not come. I had to try to earn my own admiration back first.

When I got to the starting line it was raining. I marveled at all of the lean, healthy people. They had an animal sleekness, an unfamiliar vigor in their movements. I saw a glitter of nervous self-confidence in their eyes and heard their laughing conversations as they prepared themselves to hurt. There were men and women whose springy bodies didn't seem to match the age suggested by their white hair. I looked at them with awe and wonder. In my job I did not see people like this. People like this were too busy taking good care of their bodies to go to the doctor. They felt unbelievably inspiring, unexpectedly familiar, and unbearably right.

Prior to the race, I had prepared a surprise. I knew that many race shirts celebrated their respective courses, or the sponsors of the race. But I didn't want to use my body as a bill-board for someone else's business anymore than I wanted to use my medical practice to advertise for one of the drug companies. Remembering the magical gifts he had given us growing up, I made t-shirts for my father and I to wear during the race that celebrated something I believed in.

On the front of the shirt it had the name of the race. On the back it read:

Registration: $50
Gas: $100
Hotel: $150
Running a MARATHON with MY DAD:
PRICELESS

On the back of my dad's shirt I substituted the word "SON."

The race started. My father and I loped along together in the light rain. We flowed forward with the crowd, smooth and rested. Part of me wanted to speed up, to show my father how fast I was, to try to race with his best times. With his "rebuilt" knee, my father didn't want the marathon to be a competition between us. He wanted to run it together. He wanted to lead by example. And so we ran.

We ran at a pace that allowed talking. We spoke about pain, about perseverance, about being strong. We ran and spoke about the POWs in Vietnam and how they were able to find strength to push their bodies to extremes. We spoke about my father's father, and how he had his first heart attack when he was forty-eight. People passed us, shoes making moist sounds on the wet pavement, telling us they loved our shirts. My dad told me about running his first marathon. He didn't really know why he did it. Running was simply an activity everyone he knew was doing. He told me that when he was my age every town had a marathon, even little towns like Fort Riley, Kansas. I asked him where they had all gone, what had happened to them. He frowned and said he didn't know.

We walked during a couple of parts. It was pleasantly surprising to discover that no one cared if we did. Even we didn't! It was like discovering a secret weapon that only people who had done a marathon knew was there all along.

The rain stopped. A woman with a dog ran beside us for a time. We ran to the rhythm of our breathing, our feet, and our beating hearts. The sky never did brighten much, staying the color of pewter, keeping things cool and humid all day. We ran and we talked, and we felt our bodies fatigue. We used our conversation to guide our minds so they didn't come up with their own ideas.

My friend Travis Adams, a psychologist, later told me that unlike women, men seldom just sit down to talk. To get men to talk, they need some activity to work on together to bring them close enough to talk. This could be fishing, or working on a car, playing videogames, or exercising. I found that more than the run, I reveled in the conversation and time with my dad.

Running that marathon is my favorite memory of time spent with my father: light rain falling, arms pumping, legs aching, suffering the miles together, and bearing the suffering because we were together.

After the marathon was over, I was curious about how tired I would feel. I discovered that I was tired, but not dead. I had a new sense of what was physically possible, a new sense of self-mastery and esteem through hard work. I looked at myself in the mirror. I had lost all the weight I had gained in medical school. What remained was light, and lean, the result of hundreds of miles of training.

"I am a marathoner," I whispered to the voices of self-doubt. And the voices were quiet.

When residency was over, I needed to pay the military back for the training I had received. I asked what the most difficult assignment was. I was told that a family physician was needed in Korea for a year. I volunteered for three.

We believe all things, we hope all things, we have endured many things, and hope to be able to endure all things.
If there is anything virtuous, lovely, or of good report or praiseworthy, we seek after these things.
Joseph Smith, Prophet

Sometimes it is our failure to become our perceived ideal that allows us to become unique.
Conan O'Brien, Comedian

MILE 5
(In)Credibility:
Building an Ultramarathon(er)

Koyaanisqatsi: (Hopi) (n) nature out of balance; a way of life so unbalanced that you need a new way.

Three years later my career came to a fork in the road. I could go into a practice with lighter hours that took care of a special population of individuals who were pre-screened to be healthy, or apply for a competitive academic position where I would see the sickest patients possible, do more complex procedures, deliver babies again, and work longer hours teaching at a family medicine residency program in Florida.

I only saw one road.

I experienced the rocky initiation of being the new guy. There were lectures every morning and lunch. Blistering questions were asked of the residents on every medical subject. I cringed in uncertainty over many of them myself. I had found it difficult to motivate myself to study as hard in the intervening years as I had during residency because no one was holding my feet to the fire.

Subspecialist physicians came to lecture, and left me feeling dizzy in their presence. The pulmonologists commented about blood gases that I was too embarrassed to admit I did not completely understand. The nephrologist, a brilliant physician named Dr. Dass spoke about blood salts, and how patients and physicians misunderstood the amount of salt in sports drinks before explaining a complex intracellular biochemical cascade that made me feel like the ground had dropped away under my chair. I squinted with my ears, trying to catch as much as I could, while being too embarrassed to ask questions that might reveal how little I knew.

Some of the senior residents challenged, and even corrected me on my medical decisions, citing guidelines that had not existed only three years before. Under the pressure cooker of constant correction, testing, evaluation and feedback the resident physicians grew exponentially each year. Meanwhile, I felt like I forgot more than I learned. I did not feel respected, and I wasn't sure if I respected myself. I began wrestling with one of my old demons: feeling like I wasn't smart enough, or wasn't good enough. I felt like I just wasn't quite *enough*.

"How long do you think it will be until you are discovered for the fraud that you are?" asked a familiar voice.

"You really thought you were good enough for this job? Who are you to teach other physicians?"

"Wait until they see you for who you really are," said the voices.

"You are getting old, and your mind is slow, you'll never be able to learn this stuff fast enough."

I noticed that some of the other faculty physicians had cars whose bumper stickers read "13.1," or "26.2." Though I had run a marathon, I found my self-doubts trivializing it.

"You may have run one, but you probably ran slower than everyone else."

"Yeah, probably better if you don't mention it."

"Good thing you don't have one of those bumper stickers, because people would just ask about it, and you don't want to embarrass yourself."

Patients continued to come in and the pain train roared passed me each day. I wondered if I could somehow model fitness for them, or eat better for them, or lose weight for them by proxy. I began running again to try to regain my mental balance.

One day, another faculty member, Dr. Chang, invited people in our department to join teams to run a relay race around the local bay. It was 36.8 miles long. It was divided into six sections that were roughly six miles each. As evidenced by their bumper stickers, some of my co-workers considered themselves athletes.

Six-person teams began forming and the smack talk began to flow.

I looked at the distance. It was only ten miles longer than a marathon. I remembered my surprise after finishing my marathon to discover that though I was tired, I was not *dead* tired. I remembered my father's lesson that credibility is established by playing with your troops, and slightly dominating them. Physical prowess is inherently credible. I ached to have a little credibility; to try to show my new co-workers that I was a good person, perhaps even a person worth admiring. I thought of the silhouette of my father's towering example over me. Though I hadn't yet run faster than his legacy, maybe there was another way out from under his shadow: I would not run faster, but farther.

I contacted the race director Mr. Samac. Trying to sound confident, I asked if I could run the entire thing. Mr. Samac replied that he a handful of people had already contacted him and asked him the same question. No one had been approved yet. He asked if I thought I could actually do it, and how long I thought it would take as they were hoping to wrap the whole race up around noon. I told him my estimate. He mentioned that there would be no water or food stations along the way. He asked if I had someone who could support me.

I thought of my wife. I told him I would call him back.

Katie knew of my struggles at work, and my desire to prove myself. I told her what I was thinking of doing and asked if she would help me. I needed her to drive a vehicle to carry food, liquids, and to rescue me if I got hurt. Just as I couldn't do the marathon without my father, I couldn't do this race without her.

She gave me one of those looks that is probably short, but feels really long. I could feel myself being weighed. I briefly wondered what a single unit of resolve is measured in...

Finally she took a deep breath, and said, "Sure."

I called Mr. Samac, and told him my wife would be driving my support vehicle, and she would have food and drinks for me. After some time to consider, he said okay, and let me know that there would be one other person running the entire thing. On the race registration we had to enter our team name, and the names of the people who would be running each of the six sections. For my team name I wrote "Alone," and my name on each of the six lines representing each leg of the race.

I ordered some new running shoes online and was asked if I wanted a motto custom embroidered on them. The words could be up to five letters. I thought about how people in fantasy novels frequently named their swords, musicians named their guitars, and sailors named their boats. After giving it some thought, I filled out my answers.

When they arrived a few weeks later, I pulled them from the box and tried them on. They were light and soft. On the left shoe was embroidered "DCPLN" and on the right, "PAIN." These were my two faithful running companions.

I scoured my bookshelves to find that **Whitsett and Dolgener's** old marathon book so I could review the progression chart. I copied it down and then extrapolated out another ten miles on the long runs on Saturday. I began running longer and longer runs each Saturday. By the tenth week, I ran a marathon. The following Saturday I ran twenty-eight miles. The next Saturday I ran thirty miles at a stretch, then began tapering before the race. I hoped that would be long enough to prepare me to run almost thirty seven miles. I believed that it would. Several marathon training books suggested only running twenty miles during the longest preparatory run.

At work, yet another team had formed, and I was invited to join. I declined, mentioning that I was already running it. When I was asked what team I'd be running for, I teased and said because I didn't have any friends I was going to run it by myself.

The night before the race—during registration—I asked Mr. Samac when I should start. He told me to start as early as I needed to just as long as I could be done by noon when they would have the after-party. I told him I would start at six o'clock in the morning, one hour before the relay teams.

The race was beginning and ending at a local restaurant. When I arrived the next morning, an hour before the regular race start, there was already a buzzing crowd of people in bright athletic clothing. Once again, their athleticism and energy was rejuvenating! they contrasted so sharply with the patients I saw on a daily basis. I tried to quietly check in with Mr. Samac to let him know I was going to get started. He told me that the other runner had started six hours earlier. He then quieted the entire energetic crowd.

"Hey everyone! Travis Stephensen is going to start one hour early because he is running the entire thing by himself, let's wish him luck!"

The room burst into clapping cheers, and approving nods. As I made my way out, people patted me on the back, asked how fast I was going to do it, and wished me luck.

I went outside into the dark air. The wind was crisp, scented with sand and sea salt. I started the timer on my watch, and started running. My wife leapfrogged ahead of me about four miles. As the sun rose dragging the temperature up with it, I shed my reflective belt, and eventually my shirt. My goal was to keep cold for as long as possible. The longer I could keep my body from sweating, the less I would need to drink, which would be less to weigh me down.

As I met up with my wife at the seven mile mark, I noticed that I was averaging seven minute miles. I switched shoes, ate one energy gel, and drank a bottle of Gatorade with a McDonald's salt packet in it.

I ran eighteen miles before I started getting tired. I walked up one hill, feeling worried that I was only halfway.

This was also the point closest to our house. After checking on my status, my wife detoured and went to pick up our kids to come and watch.

Meanwhile, with each passing mile, I could feel the relay teams chasing me down. They were getting faster as they replaced tired runners with fresh runners at each new leg of the relay. I knew they were back there. I could feel my one hour lead being eaten away by hungry racers. The first team passed me around mile twenty while I was in a bathroom. I don't know if his teammates told him or not, but I suspect they knew that they were the leaders of the relay racers.

At each of the transition points, more and more of the competing teams' support vehicles arrived as the runners got closer. I waved at the people from my clinic in the waiting vehicles.

The one runner ahead of me started walking certain sections, so I was able to keep just a few hundred yards behind him until we reached the marathon transition point six miles later. When I arrived there, a bunch of the people from my department were waiting for their running teammates, and they came out to greet and cheer for me.

"Well, there's a marathon," I said, walking to my wife's car to get a snack, "and I have to admit, I'm feeling kind of tired." People laughed. "I'm glad there's only ten miles to go."

As the fatigue caught up to me, so did the other teams. The last ten miles were uncomfortable. As I had learned with my long practice runs, fatigue heightened my awareness of my own body; not a particularly comfortable thing to be aware of in that state, but familiar. I was surprised to discover however, that the relationship between discomfort and distance was not linear. Because it was unknown territory, I had guessed that I would become more and more uncomfortable with each mile. That did not happen. Instead, I discovered for myself something that ultramarathoner Anne Trason had said, "It hurts up to a point, and then it doesn't get any worse."

Unlike pain, however, my speed *was* proportional to distance. My wife and kids continued to leapfrog me, shouting cheers out the windows of the minivan. Seeing me poking along, my thirteen-year-old son and ten-year-old daughter asked if they could run with me.

When I was a kid, we never dared ask to run with my father, he was simply too fast, and too busy. But I was neither too fast, nor too busy, so they began taking turns, alternating every few miles. As we neared the finish line, both kids wanted to run to the end with me. As we got closer, my friends and residents from clinic—whose team had already finished by this time—came out to run along with me. I teased them that they could try to keep up as I stiffly shuffled along. My friend Devin, an excellent physician who had also been a college football running back, started chanting, "Stephensen's a badass!" Some of the others joined in as we crossed the finish.

My kids laughed at both his language and his compliment. I could feel them recalibrating their estimation of who exactly their father was. I could feel the residents recalibrating their estimation of their new teacher. More importantly I hoped they also upgraded their estimation of who they were and what they were capable of. I had to recalibrate as well. From my toes to my back I hurt. But again, not as bad as I had imagined. My own imagination had distorted the challenge unnecessarily. I thought of other things I had turned away from because of my own intimidating imagination.

I crossed the finish line at six hours and ten minutes. My wife took a picture of me that is my single favorite photograph. My forehead had little white streaks where sweat had run and dried. My eyes look both tired and calm. Katie looked at me, smiling at my beautiful, honest exhaustion, and told me she was proud of me. It was the second time in our marriage that I remember her saying those words. The only other was the day I graduated from medical school. I started crying.

At work the following week, Dr. Dass asked me if I had been running on Saturday. I laughed and admitted that I had. He said, "I saw you when I was driving this morning, and then I saw you all the way over in town hours later, and you were still running. Then, I went to the store, and picked up my kids and I saw you hours later and you were still running. I said to my kids: this man has been running since this morning. How far did you run?"

I told him I had run all the way around the bay. He frowned and nodded, genuinely impressed. I never imagined that there was anything I could do that would impress Dr. Dass.

A couple of weeks later, someone put a bumper sticker on my car as a surprise. It read: 36.8.

"Devin, did you put a bumper sticker on my car?" I asked.

"Lots of people have stickers that say 13.1, or 26.2," he laughed, "but no one but you has a 36.8."

A few months later, my wife ran into Mr. Samac. He asked how I was doing. Katie mentioned that someone had made a bumper sticker for me. Mr. Samac asked where it came from. My wife didn't know, so she called me to ask. Devin wasn't in that day, so I googled "ultramarathon bumper sticker." Various images came up. In the midst of these was a picture of a car bumper. It was covered from right to left with bumper stickers. On the far right was a sticker that said 0.0. This was followed by one that said 5k, then 10k, then 13.1, then 26.2, then 50, then 70.3, then 100, then 140.6.

I stared at that bumper.

I kept staring.

A professional photographer once told me that at a photography contest a photo should hold a person's attention for at least four seconds before they look away. I stared at the photo of that bumper for what felt like four minutes. It struck me as the ultimate athlete's bumper, and I wanted it. It had an elegance, a completeness that called to me with the same voice the stories of adventure had used when they called to me as a kid.

*Human beings, who are almost unique in having the ability to
learn from the experience of others, are also remarkable for their
apparent disinclination to do so.*
Douglas Adams, Writer

*Concerning all acts of initiative or creation,
there is one elementary truth, the ignorance of which kills
countless ideas and splendid plans:
that the moment one definitely commits oneself,
then Providence moves too.*
William Hutchinson Murray, Mountaineer

MILE 6
Freezing Water, Finish Lines, and Founding a University

Kairos: (Greek) (n) the perfect, delicate, crucial moment; the
fleeting rightness of time and place that creates the opportune
atmosphere for actions, words, or movements; also weather.

At a Wilderness Medicine Conference I attended, a
thermophysiologist named Gordon Giesbrecht gave a presentation
about his research on cold water drowning and hypothermia. He
showed a video of one of his grad students swimming across an

icy river. As she swam past the chunks of ice toward the shore, she swam confidently making cheerful, if terse, conversation with Giesbrecht and his research team who were filming her from a canoe. When she approached the shore in the video, Professor Giesbrecht drew our attention to what was about to happen. She stopped swimming so confidently. Once she was able to feel the bottom of the river, she collapsed forward. She crawled up the shore weakly. When her arms reached the shore, she collapsed, half in the water and half out. She couldn't move. They continued to film, asking her to describe what she was feeling. She shivered so violently she could not move and could barely speak.

I was grateful I was not one of his graduate students.

Professor Giesbrecht asked us, "What happened? Why was she able to swim so confidently for so long when the water was deep, fast, and cold? Why had her strength abandoned her when the water was slow, shallow, and safety was so near?"

We shook our heads at his riddle. He then pointed out that while she was in the icy water she had adrenaline, strength and focus. It was when she could feel the bottom of the river that she relaxed. That was when she lost focus. She lost her edge and her adrenaline. Her muscles relaxed and she could barely get out of the water. The icy river was not her greatest danger, it was the shore. He pointed out that the act of rescuing someone from cold water was often the most dangerous part of the entire ordeal.

That was what I had discovered about finish lines: they weakened me. After I finished the marathon with my dad, my training motivation did not just slowly leak out of me like air from a flat tire. It was gone in a single inaudible pop. I did not run for six months. After running around the bay, I completely stopped running again. Paradoxically, in the very moment when a new door of powerful self-mastery opened, I found myself powerless to explore it any further. Like Professor Giesbrecht's students, I felt myself laying on that shore, weakened by it and unable to move.

In a way, the same thing had happened after I finished residency. I had worked so hard in college to get to medical school, and then worked so hard to get through it and get to residency. Once I was in residency, I worked horrific hours, and strained at the in-service exams and the board certification exams. And then, once residency was over, I stopped studying. I told myself I had reached the shore and I was exhausted, not realizing it was the shore that was weakening me.

Yet as I lay there, I continued to think about the photo of the car's bumper stickers: 0.0, 5k, 10k, 13.1, 26.2, 50, 70.3, 100 and 140.6. After our marathon, my dad had gone on to race in a 70.3 mile half Ironman. I tried to imagine what it would feel like to complete a 140.6 mile full Ironman. Years ago I met a man who had just returned from completing an Ironman. I looked at him in awe, asking what it was like. He had said, "Oh, you feel tired, but I believe anyone could do an Ironman."

I didn't believe it. And yet, I had to admit to myself that if *I* could run a marathon, then I was absolutely sure that anyone could. However, at my current pace, taking half a year to train, and then half a year to rest, it would take me several years to complete all of the races I hoped to complete.

There was the pesky problem of time.

Like many of my dreams—learning to play the guitar, writing a book, hiking the Appalachian Trail, having a secret door, cultivating a beautiful Asian garden—I imagined completing the bigger races when I had a great swathe of pristine, uninterrupted time; in other words during a magical period called "retirement." This was the logical equivalent to telling myself that I would swim faster once I reached the shore and the pressure was off.

Many of my patients used this same reasoning. They mentioned their busy schedules, and that they didn't have time to go to the gym. I saw the daily consequences of following that logical argument to its unhealthy end. People at work told me that they wanted to run huge distances, or get in shape, but then shrugged that they just didn't have time.

What Professor Giesbrecht's experiments demonstrated was that pressure is critical to achieving something that feels difficult. Time constraints are useful because scarcity creates valuable pressure. In surplus, time is not valued. Doing something worthwhile is never about "having" time, as if it arrives unannounced on a shining platter. If I didn't exercise when I didn't have time for it, then I wouldn't exercise when I did have time for it.

I began to realize that I have a magical ability to create time, sometimes out of thin air. I have always made time for my highest priorities. If something is important to me, I find a way. If it is not important to me, I find an excuse. What my patients were actually telling me was that health and fitness were not their priorities. "I don't have time," is the adult equivalent of "the dog ate my homework." It is just a pseudo-legitimate sounding way of saying, "It isn't important to me."

During this time I heard about an ultramarathoner and Navy SEAL named David Goggins who taught me the key to unblock my "runner's block." Goggins is a legend in the ultra-endurance sport world. He started running to raise money for the families of some of his teammates who were killed in Afghanistan.

"I could do this different ways," he said, "like carwashes or whatever, but people respond to people suffering. People respond to pain. So you have to do painful things."

So he searched on the internet for the ten most difficult feats in the world. Number one was the Badwater 135, a legendarily brutal race through Death Valley in August when the temperatures are 120-130 degrees Farenheit that is over six marathons long. When he tried to sign up, the organizers asked how many ultras he had completed, and he admitted that he had never even run a marathon. They told him to get some experience first. Four days later he ran his first hundred miler. The consequences on his body were terrible: stress fractures in both feet and muscle breakdown that threatened his kidneys. Two weeks later he ran the Las Vegas marathon. He made it to Badwater and against a field of the best ultramarathon runners in the world placed fifth. He then went on a tear of extreme endurance events, completing three marathons, thirty ultramarathons, and eventually running 2623.65 miles in thirty months. I studied him, wanting to understand how he was able to do these things, and what his thought process was like.

"I'm the kind of person who likes to do things that he doesn't like to do. I don't like running, so that kind of drives me to run."

"My life doesn't have a finish line," he says. "So, when I crossed the finish line at the Ironman it doesn't matter because I know that in two or three weeks from now I'll be doing something else to put my body through more pain. All my races, they never end. They just kind of fall in together. It's just one big journey that won't end until I die."

Gretchen Rubin wrote about the difference between a goal and a resolution. A *goal* is something that is achieved once, and can be checked off as completed, like "see the Great Wall of

China," or "have an aquarium." A *resolution* is something that we aim toward, but can never really achieve permanently or perfectly, like "have excellent manners," or, "learn to play golf." Sometimes actually achieving a goal is the least helpful thing we can do because we stop progressing and improving. David Goggins and Gordon Geisbrecht are right about finish lines. To swim through freezing waters, or run through burning deserts, we must swim beyond the shore, and run beyond the finish line. Sometimes we have to transform our goals back into resolutions to extend their usefulness. We must be vigilant about allowing a finish line, or the completion of a goal to weaken our resolve.

This paradigm even offered a solution for how I could actually do all the races I had seen on the bumper sticker. I could use one race simply as training for the next one. I would not allow myself time to be weakened by finish lines. Maybe this was what people meant when they said that life, like running, isn't about the finish line, it is about the journey.

As I committed to this idea, a plan began to materialize. I would start with the 36.8 mile run around the bay again, and use that foundation to prepare for a fifty mile ultramarathon. I would then use that to prepare for a 70.3 mile half Ironman, and finally, I would use that to prepare for a 140.6 mile full Ironman. There would be no enfeebling finish line.

The hair on my arms stood up, and my mind raced as I thought about it. It was both intimidating and exciting; inviting and scary. But when it was broken down in steps, the impossible was approachable.

I wasn't sure how much time I needed between races. How could I both recover from the previous race and increase my mileage for the next? To do this would take months, at least half a year. In honor of Whitsett and Dolgener's Marathon Class, I dubbed it my, "Semester of Endurance Experiments."

My favorite story from the writings of Ralph Waldo Emerson in his essay *Education,* offered an inspiring mental model for my semester. Emerson wrote about meeting a man in London named Sir Charles Fellowes. When Fellowes was traveling in Xanthus, a man had pointed with his staff to some carved work on the corner of a stone half buried in the soil. Fellowes scraped away the dirt, and was struck by the beauty of the sculptured stone. Looking around he saw more blocks and fragments peeking out of the soil. He returned to the spot, procured laborers and uncovered many blocks. He learned the Greek language, read history and studied ancient art to explain his stones. He hired a sculptor, experts in coins, and interested scholars and connoisseurs. In his third visit he brought back statues to England, and reconstructed marble reliefs in the British Museum. Emerson wrote, "But mark that in the task he had achieved an excellent education, and become associated with distinguished scholars who he had interested in his pursuit; in short, had formed a college for himself; the enthusiast had found the master, the master, who he sought. Always genius seeks genius, desires nothing so much as to be a pupil and to find those who can lend it aid to perfect itself."

Like Sir Charles Fellowes, I wanted to explore and make discoveries. I wanted to build a university for improving myself. In my mind I called the life I wanted to live, "The University of Me." I briefly imagined designing a college sweatshirt with this logo on it in a typical collegiate font with some sort of clever Latin motto written under it in calligraphy. I would have to think of one…

Unlike David Goggin's desire to have no finish line that compelled him to keep running and biking and swimming for years, I decided that the Semester of Endurance Experiments would only be one semester long. Though I wasn't sure what I would do after it, there are many other things I want to learn and explore, other lives I wanted to live, other versions of me I wanted to be.

I sat down to sketch out a rough plan. I wondered how much tuition would cost.

The Price of Shoes:	$89
Around the Bay Ultra:	$49
Gas:	$80
Hotel:	$60
50 miler:	$50
Bike Tune-Up:	$75
Gas:	$90
Hotel:	$120
½ Ironman:	$250
Gas:	$180
Hotel:	$82
Ironman:	$650
Total:	$1775

At one point I had imagined that to afford tuition at such a prestigious university would require some sort of wealthy benefactor, some patron of sport, some corporate sponsor. But as I looked at it, I realized that because I had done the hard things first and had a job that I could sponsor myself. We can sponsor our own dreams. I could gift myself a full-ride scholarship at the University of Me.

Within this imagined university, I designed the curriculum for my Semester of Endurance Experiments deliberately and rationally. Though I would be primarily an autodidact, I decided that like Sir Charles Fellowes, I would find and hire a faculty of subject matter experts: running coaches, ultramarathoners, a swim coach, a cycling coach, nutritionists, exercise physiologists, sports psychologists, theologians, anthropologists, human relations experts, and kinesiologists. After all, this semester would redefine my relationship with food, my thoughts, my body, my dogs, my father, my wife, my kids, myself, and my God.

This university would have a research department to design and then conduct experiments. Experiments like: how far could I run total? What shoes should I wear? How would foods affect my performance? Finally, I decided my university would also need an English department to write about and publish the results of my experiments and my dissertation.

Like most students, I didn't realize all of the real life applications for what I was studying. Nor did I realize the long term consequences that this semester would have on my career, family, or the rest of my life.

As the ideas came together, I told my wife about my plan. I told her how much of my time this semester would require after work, and on Saturdays, which was usually spent at family events. I felt like I was asking for time that belonged to her. Katie took in my excitement, steadying herself with a deep breath. I could see her silently brace her own mind under the weight of my request, testing its heft. Without smiling, but with a determination to shoulder her own semester-long endurance event, she said yes.

I moved on to the third and final step in my plan. The year after my father and I had run the marathon he had kept exercising and had gone on to complete his first 70.3 mile half Ironman. After speaking with my wife I looked forward to the conversation with my father all week. This semester was an answer to his charge. I was still paying attention to his example, still working to be a good man he had charged me to become. I wanted to put it in terms he would like, so I thought about framing the semester to show that I was trying to keep that fifth commandment about honoring my parents. I hoped his work schedule would allow him to do at least half of the events with me.

I bit my lip. Maybe just as I had gotten him back to running marathons, I could get him to complete an Ironman, something I knew he had thought about for years. As he got older, and approached the age when many of my patients started having heart attacks, I secretly thought I could somehow protect him by turning him back into the super athlete of my childhood. In my mind I imagined his doubts, and that maybe he wouldn't want to. But in the very least I heard him say, "I'm proud of you son for trying to do something great," or, "Wow son, an Ironman! I know you can do it!"

When I finally told my father about my planned Semester of Endurance Experiments, he listened quietly to my excited plan, and the time it would require and how I would use one race to prepare for the next one. Then he said simply, "Well, remember you have responsibilities to your family as well."

When he said those words, I suddenly went deaf, and the movie my kids were watching went silent. I could feel the phone still vibrating with his voice but I could feel the jaws of loneliness and sadness close around me and swallow.

People often say that motivation doesn't last.
Well, neither does bathing.
That's why we recommend it daily.
Zig Ziglar, Author

Whatever you think you can do or believe you can do, begin it—
for action has magic grace and power in it.
Goethe, Philosopher

MILE 7
Brick Wall Preliminaries

Sciamachy: (Greek) (n) a battle between imaginary enemies; fighting your shadow.

After my conversation with my father, my enthusiasm limped along wounded and skittish with uncertainty. I was sitting at my desk working to resuscitate my crazy dream when I heard the sound of old boots and familiar voices approaching me from behind.

"What are you planning there?"

I tried to cover the spreadsheet of my Semester of Endurance Experiments training program. Using the training plan I had developed the previous year, I was extrapolating it out for the entire semester. I had been carefully calculating the percent increase in mileage each week, trying not exceed what I assumed was my body's speed limit for adaptation.

"Hey, look at this! He thinks he's going to be an Ironman!"

I hate the sound of their grating laughter.

"Need we remind you why that is not going to happen?"

I exhaled slowly. I hate the voices of my doubts, but can't seem to shake them.

"Look at you; you're not built like an athlete. You're all elbows and ribs. You don't have time to train like a professional athlete. You didn't even play any sports in college. Who the heck are you?"

"Yeah," added the other voice. I always have two voices of self-doubt for some reason; probably so I can hear them in stereo. "You are thirty-seven years old, way past your prime."

"You don't know what you're doing. You're probably going to tell people about this, thinking the extra attention will help 'hold you accountable to achieve your dreams,' but all that will do is just add one more person's laughing voice when you totally fail. Go ahead, tell everyone what you're planning so they think you're really hot stuff, that way more people are watching when you make a total fool of yourself!"

"Hey, even if you don't fail, you'll probably get hurt. Just look at the number of people who get hurt trying to train for a marathon. You'll probably have some terrible bike accident and develop chronic pain like your favorite patients."

They elbow each other and laugh their coarse, barking laughs.

"Yeah, when are you even going to have time to do all of this?"

I get tired of them. "I'll have you know that I'm going to start riding my bike to work."

This just makes them laugh even harder.

I had bought my bike from a friend of my father's seven years before, and at the time it was about seven years old. The man I bought it from had been doing triathlons until he had hurt his back. So he quit training and instead, at the age of fifty, took up smoking. I had replaced the pedals with the stirrup pedals from my father's old bike.

"You know you're gonna get a flat tire, and be late for work."

"I know how to change a flat, and besides, I can call my wife to come get me if I have to."

"She's gonna be pissed off."

"No," I said, "she's not."

"We'll see, but even if she isn't, you'll get home all tired and grumpy. See how long she supports you then."

Laughter.

"I'm not going to come home grumpy."

"Yeah sure you won't. And you won't be tired after riding twenty-four miles either. You'll probably be falling asleep at your desk at work. See how your bosses like that!"

I stared at the spreadsheet I was making, trying to ignore them.

"Where you gonna park that crotchety old thing?"

"What are you gonna wear? You don't even own any snazzy spandex."

"You'll get stuck in the rain."

"It's dark outside all the time, how will anyone see your bike in the dark?

"Where are you gonna shower at work?"

"What are you gonna do about clean clothes at work?"

"What about food?"

"How are you gonna train for a 2.4 mile swim in your thirty foot unheated pool in the middle of winter?"

Seeing I am not answering their questions, just clenching my jaw and staring straight ahead, they switch tactics.

"Hey, even if you ride as carefully as you can, you can't control how the cars behave. You spend enough time on the road and you will probably get hit by a car. The hospital chief of staff got hit riding his bike to work just a couple of years ago."

"Yeah, and you remember that mountain biker you saw in the ER after his bike accident? You will probably break your neck and end up paralyzed. Just like him."

Then, one leaned in real close. I could smell his bitter breath with each word. "Is it really worth it?"

I tried not to let my excuses know they were getting to me, but each question was like a rock being thrown into a calm pond. I could feel doubt ripple through my mind.

And so, as a prerequisite for my main courses, I decided to become a student of my own excuses and doubts, hoping it would help me unravel their causes.

"Doubt-ology is not even a real word."

"Shush!"

Where did all these doubts, anxiety, excuses and fears come from? Were they from my parents? Was I trying to compete with my father, and so part of me was sabotaging the whole semester to protect him? Did they happen because he wasn't excited about the whole thing? Were they simply the questioning voices of my mother I had internalized and thought were my own? Were they left over from competing with seven siblings for parental attention? Some vestigial habit from sabotaging each others' attempts at parental attention that I was now displacing to sabotage myself? Were these simply the regurgitation of the thousands of excuses I had heard from all the overweight patients I saw day in and day out for years? Were they from genetic madness? Addiction, bipolar and even schizophrenia run in my family. Were they manifestations of my religious beliefs? Some twisting of humility into humiliation? Was it possible to be both confident and humble at the same time? Did my anxiety serve an evolutionary purpose? Maybe having a constantly worrying mind kept my ancestors sharp and alert. Was anxiety from too little serotonin? Or too much adrenaline? Was there something in my food? Did I eat doubts and digest excuses with my American diet? Was my American culture weakening me? Were self-doubts simply the price of allowing myself to think too much? Is 'thinking too much' even possible? I made a mental note to try to figure that out later.

I sat back and looked at my list. What a surprising number of suspects had been caught in my mental sting operation!

But, just as I could hear these voices of self-doubt, and self-consciousness, I had collected other voices too: gentle encouraging voices.

When he was diagnosed with pancreatic cancer and told he had six months to live, Professor Randy Pausch thought about what final message he wanted to leave with his students, family and the world. I read his book, The Last Lecture, where he summed up his life philosophy: follow your childhood dreams. He suggested that there was a reason that certain things captivate us as kids and call to us. One of the keys he taught as a warning to his audience was that there are always brick walls around our dreams.

Always.

But, the brick walls aren't there to keep us away from our dreams. They are there to keep other people away from them. They are there for us to prove to ourselves and to the Universe how deeply we want to achieve our dreams. Scaling brick walls is how we develop our strength, our courage, and our ingenuity. For every doubt, and every obstacle to my dream, I would have to find a solution. This wasn't going to just be months of physical training, I would have to become mentally stronger too. And wasn't that precisely what I had wanted? The Semester of Endurance Experiments wasn't composed of four races. It was composed of thousands of events. My doubts and my dreams raced each other every day on different courses, often through courses with surprise events.

For example: I had put off signing up for Ironman Texas—the closest race that was not on a Sunday—while waiting for a separate financial commitment to resolve. The entry fee was $650 dollars. When the other problem was solved, I found I had missed the chance to register. The race was full. The only open Ironman events were on Sundays, or else four months later. The doubts started laughing. They had checkmated me, blocking me from the key event.

I looked up at the heavens and said a defiant little prayer.

"Let the record show that I showed up. I was ready to do this whole thing. And I was trying to do it without breaking the bank or that commandment about the Sabbath either."

During my weekly phone call to my dad, I told him of my discouragement. I had been so excited about the whole thing just a few weeks before. Now I didn't see how I could do it.

My father mentioned that he had been looking for another half ironman triathlon to do. Maybe we could do that?

"I already looked. The only half Ironman in Florida is all booked up."

"What about the other brands?"

"What do you mean?"

"That one I did a few years ago, it wasn't an Ironman brand event. There are other events put on by other companies that are the same distance, they just can't use the brand name."

"Wait, you mean they have half Ironman races that are the same distance?"

"Yes."

"Do they have full Ironman races?"

"Oh, I'm sure they do. You'll just have to look around the internet a little and find one."

I smiled.

"Thank you Dad!"

"If it isn't an Ironman, it isn't an Ironman," said a familiar voice.

"If it isn't a marathon, it isn't…wait. What? Is it the brand, or *the distance* that contains the truth about myself that I am seeking?"

No answer.

"That's what I thought."

I found a "half" distance triathlon that wasn't fully booked and it was in my own state, in the month right when I needed it to be. And then, I found a "full" distance triathlon. It was in Texas, on a Saturday, a month earlier than the other one, and was two hundred dollars cheaper.

The view from on top of the brick wall made me smile again.

Once I had answered this strange call, once I had really committed to this semester and done my part, it felt like God, or the Universe was conspiring with me to achieve these impossible goals. Shortly after I finished my plan, construction teams finished building a brand-new bike path near the hospital. Maybe God likes to help us achieve our goals, but maybe He wants to see us prove how bad we want things too. Probably not to prove it to Him, but to ourselves.

As I completed building my training program, and really put myself into the effort, I found that the excuses were still there. Just as my imagination helped me plan, I began to realize that I could misuse my imagination and worry. My resolve and my doubts continued their fierce internal competition. When I woke up with dread because it was raining, or it was cold, I had to work to find a reason to go out there and train that was even bigger than the doubts. As I worked to discipline the thoughts that did not make me strong, I discovered I could not simply empty my mind of doubts; I had to address them legitimately.

With practice, I began winning more and more of these other races, these preliminaries. I began making myself stronger than my doubts, stronger than my excuses.

We run to undo the damage we've done to body and spirit.
We run to find some part of ourselves yet undiscovered.
John "The Penguin" Bingham, Run/Walker

Suddenly all my ancestors are behind me.
Be still, they say. Watch and listen.
You are the result of the love of thousands.
Linda Hogan, Poet

MILE 8
The Primal Present

Querencia: (Spanish) (n) a place from which one's strength is drawn, where one feels at home; the place where you are your most authentic self.

In his book *Finding Ultra*, Rich Roll wrote about his wife Julie who is an artist. If someone asked how long it had taken her to paint a gorgeous canvas, her reply was: "My whole life."

As people found out what I was doing they asked how long I had been training. I began to allow myself to answer, "My whole life." Though it had only been a semester, everything that had happened to me up to this point had shaped me: running in cross country in high school, my poor PT test performance when I arrived at residency, deciding to take my fitness more seriously, the confidence that came with running a marathon with my dad.

If I want to be completely honest, however, my training actually began before I was born. It was shaped, after all, by my father's decisions, by his training, and by his example.

Then again, I could look even further back. I could say that my father ran because his father did not. He had started having heart attacks in his forties.

It reminded me of one of a story from addiction recovery. One brother asks the other, "Why do you drink?"

And the brother answers, "Because Dad was an alcoholic. How come you don't drink?"

And the first brother says, "Because Dad was an alcoholic."

As the semester progressed, I was trying to reverse engineer my own human design. I wanted to know why my body has the shape that it does. Claiming I had been running my whole life, or that it began with my father, or even his father, were all gross over-simplifications. My training as a runner actually began hundreds and even thousands of years before I was even born.

Christopher McDougal popularized the anthropological theory known as the Running Man Theory in his book <u>Born to Run</u>. Initially developed by Drs. David Carrier and Dennis Bramble, this theory tried to explain how it was that long before humans developed tools to hunt, they hunted. They did this not with claws or fangs. They did it by running their prey into heat exhaustion.

Generation after generation, our ancestors ran after running animals who sometimes outran them. Over generations, this race for survival, this winning and losing chiseled and shaped the bodies of both hunter and hunted. Carrier and Bramble found a total of twenty-six different adaptation on the human body that are used to make us more efficient long-distance runners. Feet elongated and arched becoming longer, more efficient levers for prying ourselves off of the ground. Toes shortened. Legs stretched until humans were basically two long muscled, springy legs with a short body perched on top. Tendons, like the Achilles, store kinetic energy as springs and release it again without burning any calories. Four-legged running animals have diaphragms that are compressed when their guts are shoved forward by their hind legs. This arrangement allows them to only take one breath per stride. But by putting our human lungs up above our guts we are able to take multiple breaths per running stride. Even our enormous butt muscles are only used when running. Chimpanzees can't run; they have flat butts. So do non-runners.

Being covered with hair, most mammals can only cool themselves by panting. Humans, however, can cool ourselves by evaporative cooling through our ability to sweat. In fact, one of the adaptations of regular exercise is that with training, we sweat sooner, larger amounts, and more efficiently by losing less salt. Of all running accessories, sweat is the most beautiful. Exercise is simply the means that allows all that liquid awesomeness to leak out of our pores.

McDougal cited other fascinating evidence. The run times of finishers of the New York City marathon finishers shows that humans get faster each year from the youngest runners at age nineteen until their peak at age twenty-seven. After twenty-seven, speeds decline. However, to become as slow as they were when they were nineteen takes until the runners are sixty four! Faula Singh ran a marathon when he was a hundred years old. Our ability to run can potentially last for our entire lives.

We are the descendants of winners. Thousands and millions of winners. Over millennia, the human shape was developed as the ultimate endurance running animal on earth. We did nothing to earn these adaptations; they are a gift from our ancestors.

After Carrier and Bramble published their theory, they were met with some criticism because no one had ever seen a human run an animal into the ground on foot. Then, they got a phone call from a man named Louis Liebenberg in South Africa.

He explained that not only was it possible to run animals into heat exhaustion on foot, but that a tribe he had studied had done it. On average it took between three and five hours to complete a persistence hunt. It takes three to five hours of running in the sun to run an animal to death. Though I didn't chase any big animals, I did find that I could run my dogs into the ground in around that same amount of time.

That is about the same amount of time it takes to run a marathon. A marathon distance was first defined as the distance that the ancient Greek messenger Pheidippides ran from the Battle of Marathon to Athens to deliver a message before he passed out and died of heat exhaustion. It was the distance an ancient man could run before he died from heatstroke. So the margin between when an animal could be run to the ground and die of heatstroke, and when a human would suffer the same consequence was narrow. The gap between predators and prey is always narrow. Even when we are chasing our dreams.

Once it was defined as the distance that would kill someone if they actually ran it, people naturally wanted to run marathons.

Maybe that is why running hurts, because it is about killing. Long ago it might be about killing a weaker animal, but now it is about killing weaknesses in ourselves. Sometimes it is about running a big hairy audacious goal into submission—persistence hunting a dream.

Many times as I continued my training, I imagined the ghosts of lean, sinewy cavemen running and gliding alongside me. I imagined them dripping with cooling sweat on an expanse of sun-loving skin. I imagined them running for mile after mile holding the same steady pace, a pace that they could hold forever without tiring. I imagined these running ghosts trying to show me how to use all of the features of this body I had inherited.

"Look, do you see how your head is steady like a running horse, and like a running wolf, and like the other running animals? This is because you have a nuchal ligament that steadies it when you run. Walking animals don't have this. This is one of our presents for you!"

"Listen, do you hear the rhythm of your lungs breathing to the beat of your steps? Can you hear your heart drumming happily in your ears? Do you notice how your ears hear things approaching behind that you cannot see? This is one of our presents for you!"

"Feel the strength of your body. Do you feel how your shoulders swing freely and smoothly while you can keep looking forward? This is one of our presents for you!"

I ran and trained and imagined that there were specific, named individuals who had been the first with each of these amazing adaptations. I ran in the rain and imagined my cavemen ancestors checking out the butts of the available cavewomen and recognizing that some of them were much better runners. I imagined their incredible effort at seducing the owner of those genes to mix with his so that I could inherit this physical legacy. I ran up hills and imagining some of them sacrificing themselves to protect their children and the superior genes they now carried.

As I ran down dark sidewalks under the stars, I wondered if they were watching me from Caveman Heaven. Were they pointing at my stride, at my feet? Elbowing each other at what features I had of theirs? Were they pleased with what I had done with the body they had risked everything to shape, the body they had spent their lives to develop? Did my run make them proud, or were they ashamed of what I was doing with their tremendous gifts?

What about all the people who weren't taking good care of their bodies? So many of us forget who we are, and where we came from. When we forget our ancestors, we forget pieces of our own souls. Jack Donovan wrote, "Imagine the disgust and contempt our ancestors would have for us all if they lined up modern men on the street." We have forgotten that the blood of warriors runs in our veins.

It is difficult, but not impossible, to find humans who still live in conditions similar to those in which our ancestors developed.

McDougal also wrote about a group of Native Americans called the Tarahumara. They live in the Copper Canyons of Mexico and routinely run ultramarathons. They run for hours and hours, sometimes all night. Ten, twenty, fifty, a hundred miles. No problem. In the ultra-running world, they are legendary for their almost god-like endurance. People like this still exist, but they are so uncommon they seem super-human.

Across the border, living in the United States, is another group of Native Americans called the Pima. Having no history of domestic animals to use as transportation, they also had a heritage and culture of running enormous distances. But as technology developed, they stopped running. They started driving instead and started eating the easy calories of the American Diet. Like Professor Geisbrecht's grad student, they had reached the shore where effort was no longer required. The pressure to run to survive was gone, and it absolutely eviscerated their health. The Pima gained enormous weight and they also became legendary, but not for endurance. They have the unenviable distinction of the highest per capita rates of diabetes in the United States, and probably in the world.

Joseph Campbell once said, "Gods suppressed become devils." Like the Tarahumara, the Pima were born with a god-like potential to run. But when they didn't claim it, when they suppressed this god, it turned into a ruthless devil that rotted their bodies while they were still living in them. Half of all adult Pima now have diabetes. It ravages their kidneys, leaving them dependent on dialysis to filter their blood. It destroys their eyes, leaving them, in one of illness' many symbolic gestures, blind. It destroys their blood vessels and nerves, leading their beautiful, god-like feet to crumble, and decay, and require amputations.

In *The Wizard of Oz,* Dorothy had the secret to returning home in her ruby slippers. They were on her feet the whole time. For the Pima the solution is also on their feet. For my patients, and for America, the solution is on our feet. Sadly, as their bodies swell, their feet—the very solution to their problem—are slowly whittled away. As the saying goes, "It's not that diabetes runs in your family, it is just that no one in your family runs."

In the words of weightlifting coach Mark Rippetoe, "Over and above any considerations of performance for sports, exercise is the stimulus that returns our bodies to the conditions for which they were designed. Humans are not physically normal in the absence of hard physical effort."

Life is difficult. But we are the heirs of the ancients who left us an incredible legacy woven into the fabric of our own bodies and the latent strength to unlock it. As I ran through fog and mist, I felt nostalgic for a past I could not return to. I felt like a blind man who didn't know where he had come from, where he was going, where his countrymen were going, or his own children. I wished I could find an actual contemporary caveman who would teach me about this running animal gift I had inherited.

I sighed because I couldn't find one to be my running guide. So I tried to use my run as a way of honoring my mighty ancestors, as a votive candle in the darkness.

Pat Shipman, a retired professor of anthropology at Pennsylvania State University, wrote a book about how our ancestors were able to out-compete our bigger, stronger cousins the Neanderthals. His hypothesis was that we had symbiosis with a powerful ally that gave us a durable competitive advantage.

So, though I couldn't find an actual caveman, my ancestors did leave me this other gift to help me decode my buried legacy: their ancient ally and best friend.

Run, for your life, for your joy,
for your calm and peace of mind.
Run. Because your legs are strong
and your lungs are aching for the taste of air. Run.
Tyler Knott Gregson, Poet

You can lead a human to facts,
but you cannot make him think.
Dog, Professor of Animal Kinesiology

MILE 9
Guide Dogs for the Blind

Gokotta: (Swedish) (n) the act of rising in the early morning to watch the birds or to go outside to appreciate nature; literally "dawn picnic to hear the first birdsong."

As my training continued, I began running eleven miles to work and back. I felt like I had inherited a powerful but foreign sports car from wealthy, deceased relatives, and there were only confusing "modern" directions on how to use it.

"To master your own body, you need special scientifically engineered shoes, socks, and exercise clothes."

"Your body will run better if you put scientifically engineered, colored, sweetened fluids and lumps of sweetened gunk into the fuel tank."

"To master your body, hire a certified coach who has a credential stamped on a piece of parchment-colored paper."

Though I don't have anything specific against scientifically engineered things, or education, I can be a bit of a Luddite because of how quickly things change. I was simply after a different kind of knowledge. In the Nicomachean Ethics, Aristotle taught about a type of wisdom known as *phronesis* which could be contrasted with the type of wisdom that would later be called "science." Phronesis is commonly translated as "practical wisdom." People with phronesis were the master craftsmen who, when the engineer came with his mathematically derived designs, would explain why, in the real world, they wouldn't work. They didn't need training certificates. They had real world practical wisdom: street cred.

As I was trying to build up the endurance of my body to its genetic potential, I kept encountering situations where people without education seemed wiser than those who had it. But I couldn't always tell where it came from.

In her book, *The Happiness Project*, Gretchen Rubin wrote that she wanted to find and imitate a spiritual master. I did too! I wanted mine to have a practical, down to the feet, down-to earth phronesis kind of wisdom. But, to be honest, I didn't really want to spend any more time with people. Sometimes people energize me, but, like most introverts sometimes people leave me feeling drained and tired. On these long runs I was learning that many times I preferred my own thoughts and company to that of others. I was practicing to not mind my own company. I was increasing in confidence in what I brought to my mental conversations.

I wanted a teacher, but I didn't really want another person in my life. I felt like a blind man. I needed help to find these craggy contours and edges of myself without getting hurt. I wanted to find the blurry and bleeding edges of my own fatigue, of my own design. I wanted to find what was real. If I was a blind man, maybe I needed a Seeing Eye dog.

I looked at my dogs.

They looked back at me, tails wagging in smile-shaped crescents. Okay, maybe I needed two Seeing Eye dogs...

On our long Saturday runs together I listened to music. One day, the song Gone, Gone, Gone by Phillip Phillips came on just as my dogs were both looking back over their shoulders at me. It felt as if it contained the words and the rhythm that my crazy dogs would sing if they could. Sometimes the words got stuck in my head and would appear even when they weren't around.

When life leaves you high and dry,
I'll be at your door tonight.
If you need help, if you need help.

The first of our two dogs was adopted by my wife and kids after I returned from deployment. I was out of town for a month doing obstetrics. While I was delivering babies, my family welcomed a new life into our home. She was adopted from a local shelter. When my family entered the shelter, many of the dogs started barking and charging the fences. My wife was drawn to the medium sized black dog that sat quietly and looked intently at my wife's face while other dogs snarled around her cage.

When enemies are at your door,
I'll carry you away from war.
If you need help, if you need help.
Your hope dangling by a string
I'll share in your suffering,
To make you well, to make you well.

The shelter told my wife that the dog was half Labrador and half Great Dane. When they told me about the dog they had adopted, my kids were undecided on a name. I thought of the little baby I had just delivered, and suggested her name: Pyper. The name stuck.

When I returned from my trip, I noticed that this dog named Pyper was not half Great Dane.

She was half Pit Bull.

People had come to the shelter. They had seen her Pit Bull head and white chest. Then, relying on pre-formed opinions, decided she was dangerous. But through deception on the part of the shelter, and ignorance on the part of my wife, Pyper was given a chance to be judged based on her behavior. Pyper's gentle calmness shamed me of my former breed prejudices. But she still suffers from "breed profiling" many places we go.

Carl Jung once said, "Everything that irritates us about others can lead us to an understanding of ourselves." This certainly applied to my interactions with my patients. Thinking about Carl Jung's quote, I would add "Everything we love in others can also lead us to an understanding of ourselves."

The doorway through which a dog enters our lives is a reflection of our values. I had wanted a Belgian Mallinois, the Ferrari of military working dogs. They are athletic, ambitious, intelligent, and fearless. They are also expensive. They represented my urge to have the latest and the greatest.

When I looked at Pyper for the first time, I saw in her eyes what my wife had seen. They seemed to say, "I may not have a perfect family blood line, but my heart can love perfectly."

Give me reasons to believe.
That you would do the same for me.
And I would do it for you, for you.
Baby, I'm not moving on
I'll love you long after you're gone.

My wife had been abandoned as a helpless, defenseless infant by her birth mother in Korea. A few years ago we made a pilgrimage with our children to visit the White Lily Orphanage. Katie has a picture of herself as an infant with a Korean nun named Sister Maria. When her own mother had abandoned her, this woman was there, with love ready and large enough to fill the void. Katie had returned with her father when she was fourteen, and had another picture taken with Sister Maria. When we went back as adults, we showed the nuns the picture. They spoke softly to themselves as they recognized her. They indicated that Sister Maria was now quite old, and was in the hospital. We waited while the other nuns called her.

In its own way, the phone call was like a prayer. We had so many unanswerable questions. And we didn't know if she would even answer.

Finally, the nuns handed the phone to my wife. Katie said hello.

In a tired, but soft and far-away voice Sister Maria asked my wife one question: "Are you happy?"

My wife started crying. She looked at us watching her, and she thought about her life. Finally she said, "Yes. I am happy."

Sister Maria said, "Good. That is what is most important."

I believe that if we could have called Katie's actual birth mother, or even God, the question would have been the same.

You will never sleep alone.
I'll love you long after you're gone.
And long after you're gone, gone, gone.

When we were dating, in a moment of incredible vulnerability, Katie had asked me once, "Do you think your family minds that I am not white?"

Being judged by appearances affected the way people treated my wife and kids. It affects their perceptions of Pyper. Breed profiling against her is painful, just as racial profiling hurts my wife and other minorities. Abandonment is a painful thing. It tore a jagged hole in my wife's heart, and Pyper entered our lives through that hole's doorway: the love for the abandoned.

Our second dog, Paisly, entered our lives through a different doorway. She entered our lives through the door of love I leave open for my younger brother. He and his wife had bought this little puppy from a breeder. They soon found that despite the daily walks and runs, her energy level created strain in their marriage. My sister-in-law was working on her doctoral thesis, and this irrepressible puppy was doing everything in her power to compete for time and attention. Like a bottled hurricane, she was proving impossible to contain. So, in a moment of sadness and wanting to ensure she would be loved, my brother called me and asked if I could take her. Without hesitation, I said "Yes."

When you fall like a statue,
I'm goin' be there to catch you.
Put you on your feet, you on your feet.
And if your well is empty,

Not a thing will prevent me.
Tell me what you need, what do you need?

Paisly is half Labrador, and half Weimaraner. As I read about the latter breed, I found that they had been bred to run alongside horses, that they had been bred specifically to have great endurance. Because of this, the guide warned, Weimaraners have tremendous persistence. This helps them keep running when other dogs would have quit. This gift, if suppressed, could become a curse if they did not have a healthy outlet for it. Their virtuous *persistence* would be renamed as malicious *stubbornness*. This character trait that had been bred into her as a strength was the very quality that was driving my sister-in-law crazy. Sources of strength can become sources of weakness. Gods suppressed become devils.

Fortuitously, when we got Paisly, I was just starting to train. In the beginning, as the mileage increased, their pads blistered, or wore through. Then, they hardened.

Having no sense of how far we were going, or how to pace themselves, Pyper and Paisly would launch off the front porch dragging me along for the ride. At the end of their leashes, they fly like two kites. Kites made of sixty pounds of joyous, straining muscle and fur. And so begins a conversation, conducted entirely via body language and a series of Morse code like tugs on their leashes that went something like this:

"Dogs, slow down," I yank. "We have a long way to go."

"We can't slow down; it feels too good to run! We want to run this fast forever."

"Dogs, we have to pace ourselves. Trust me, I once ran a marathon, and I once ran around the entire bay, and we're training for huge runs."

"Dogs like to run marathons too!" they insist, pulling at the leashes, collars sunk tight against their muscled necks. "Only we do it while also pulling a sled. You can be our sled!"

"We'll see who drags who," I yank back on their collars "I am going to run you two into the ground."

"We love to run! We still remember our animal side. We know what we were designed to do." They smile, perfect canine smiles with soft eyes, and lolling tongues.

"You were designed to respect the biggest wolf in the pack. I will show you who that is, and who is the sled."

And so we run. They fly ahead, dragging me over the asphalt sidewalks and suburbs for the first mile. I weave leashes from hand to hand as dogs switch positions and formations around me. After two miles, they stop pulling and just run. After three miles, Pyper slows down and runs beside me. Paisly looks over her shoulder at us. After six miles, she slows and runs at my side, and Pyper falls behind us. Occasionally I catch Paisly looking up at me. When we are finally done with our long runs, I am dragging them. When we get home, they plop down on the cool kitchen tile panting and smiling beautiful canine smiles at me.

"Now who is the sled?" I ask them.

I surrender honestly.
You've always done the same for me.
So I would do it for you, for you.
Baby, I'm not moving on,
I'll love you long after you're gone
And long after you're gone, gone, gone.

My dad ran with dogs, my grandparents and great-grandparents had dogs. Dogs have been running with our human family for thousands of years and millions of miles. They are man's most ancient animal friend, the very first animal to be domesticated. Though in their case, there is some thought that they chose our company as much as we chose theirs. Dogs have always had a gift of finding the people who need them.

Maybe everyone needs an animal guide to lead them back from the cerebral lives in our heads to the animal lives in our own bodies. For running, I had two crazy guides. I wondered if any other blind people walked with two guide dogs. If you have dogs in stereo, does it give you binocular vision?

You're my back bone.
You're my cornerstone.
You're my crutch when my legs stop moving.
You're my head start.
You're my rugged heart.
You're the pulse that I've always needed.
Like a drum, baby, don't stop beating.
Like a drum baby, don't stop beating.
Like a drum baby don't stop beating.

I looked at these majestic animals who love to run. They wanted a job. So, during the Semester of Endurance Experiments at the University of Me they were appointed as Dog Professors of Animal Kinesiology. Partly because I couldn't find anyone else who wanted to run with me, and partly because I liked the acronym it made. It is a tenured, lifetime appointment.

If I could be half the person my dog is,
I'd be twice the human I am.
Charles Yu, Writer

Wait, who rescued who?
Pyper and Paisly, My Dogs

MILE 10
Love is a Four-Legged Word

Petrichor: (Greek roots) (n) the smell outside after it rains.

Sometimes I just needed to disconnect from humans and their empty commitments to try to exercise and refresh myself in the company of beings who loved to run. The origins of their enthusiasm were so foreign and so fascinating, that as we ran I watched them to try to discern its patterns.

So, in addition to paying attention to my stomach, my knees, my doubts, the skin of my feet, etcetera. I began paying attention to my dogs. Over the miles and miles I read them. In doing so, I began to decipher the curriculum they were trying to teach me.

My father had taught me that credibility with soldiers, scouts, and sons is earned with by hard physical work. The same is true with dogs. And so we ran. I noticed my dogs behaved better when exercised. Without exercise, my dogs become annoying, bothersome, and partly wild again. So do I. My thoughts, in particular become wilder. In episode after episode of his television show, Cesar Milan, the dog whisperer, demonstrated this. He would arrive at a family's home with a troubled dog situation and address the dog's bizarre behavior with exercise. He pointed out that a dog without exercise is not normal, that depriving them of exercise is a form of animal abuse. Without exercise to drain and channel their energy, dogs' pent-up energy leads to destructive and even deviant behaviors. My wife began asking which days I would be running, and thanked me for taking the dogs because they were much easier to be around when they were worthily tired. The drama and trauma of washing the dogs diminished when I ran with them in the rain.

My dogs taught me that exercise should be loved with the pure simplicity of a little kid who gets to go outside to play and love the world. When I put on my running shoes, or even open my drawer to get my socks and running shorts, my dogs wake-up and run to watch. Their sleek, muscled bodies start breathing faster, and they start pacing and circling around me, like fury charged particles circling a nucleus. Dogs don't run for time or distance, for medals or bumper-stickers. Dogs run because they remember something primal and important that humans forget in all our noise and haste: exercise is spiritual. Dogs run because it feels awesome to move, and because the world is an awesome place to explore! Our bodies feel best when they are exhausted in good causes. A dog doesn't care if you are running from your fears, or running to your dreams. If you are running, they will run with you, unafraid and dreaming only of running with you. They enjoy it so much I don't believe they have any concept of "having to" run, they only "get to" run. If offered a treat or a run, they will always choose the run.

When we are kids we call exercise "play," like a "playground." But when we are adults we call it "work," as in, "working out." This semantic shift adds a certain dignity to it, but at the cost of draining joy and wonder. I often pondered what word dogs use for exercise. I don't think they call it, "taking a walk," or merely, "going" for a run. I believe they call it "high-speed exploring!"

As they explored, they reminded me that I too, am a constituent of nature. After years of living in-doors, driving, studying, sitting, reading, listening, and clicking at a computer, it was wonderful to be outside my cubicle. The weather made me feel connected to the earth, and part of it. My dogs reminded me that as a human animal I am part of nature, so I should pay attention to it because it is my home. When I took them to a new trail, or a new neighborhood, they seemed at home even if they had never been there before.

As I trained, I started checking the weather every day because I was now subject to it. During our miles of runs, I saw clouds and stars, and more sunrises and sunsets than at any time in my life. I saw mornings so foggy that the boats at the dock looked like they were sailing through clouds. When I ran at night, I imagined myself running straight up, into the stars. I crunched frost under my feet, and felt rain sting my eyes.

Initially, I dreaded rainy days. But with practice I learned not to fear running on rainy days. There was something satisfying knowing that I was out running when others were afraid. It gave me confidence in the weather resistance and waterproofing of my own skin. Running any given route in the rain made me feel stronger and more confident than covering the same route on a sunny day. I learned rain is my friend. The wind is my friend. Hills are my friends. Cold weather is my friend. Anything that opposed me was actually helping me to become stronger. If I had no opposition, I would be weak. Many people only pay lip service to enjoying nature, but they don't really enjoy it. They hide from the sun, from the rain, from the wind, from the darkness. They hide from the strength required to live there, to thrive there.

Besides my connection with weather, my dogs also taught me to look for other animals. Mainly because they would chase these animals, I became more vigilant and aware. I learned to recognize their body language tightening when one had seen a cat, or another person walking a dog, or, worst of all, if they had found a squirrel. I learned to hate squirrels with as much intensity as they love them. I began to realize that my dogs did not necessarily have a detecting advantage on me, sometimes I would find animals first. My vision and hearing are as good as theirs. As I paid attention to what my dogs were focusing on, I began to see more. I saw deer and snakes, frogs, and osprey carrying fish in their talons. I imagined each of these animals living up to their full animal athletic (and metaphorical) potential. I saw foxes sliding into the foggy woods. I wondered what my dogs thought of having wild contemporaries living in our neighborhood. It would be like having cavemen neighbors who still lived next-doors eating grubs. We chased a family of masked raccoons walking in a hunched-backed line. Wild turkeys looked at me as I rode my bike past the field where they gathered. An owl flew passed us one night, only yards from our breathing, heaving little pack. We stopped, held our breath, and ears straining against the impossible silence of such large beating wings as it disappeared back into the darkness. One day we saw a goat prancing neatly down the suburban road puzzling all of us with its presence and queer, vertically slotted eyes. Some days we saw vultures, patiently circling black banners waving at the funeral of some animal. One morning the flipper of a manatee broke the glass reflection of the sunrise to wave at me. I learned that after every rain the turtles migrate. Rain was not an inconvenience to them; it was just a thin river in which to travel. I imagined some ancient tribal myth teaching that turtles caused the rain.

I noticed how colors changed in the rain, and I wondered how the rain affected smells. To a dog, smells tell stories about the past. A dog's nose detects what had walked that place before, and how long ago. Smells change over time as things dry, so they can smell some ways into the past. On cold sharp winter nights when I let them out, my dogs would stop and lift their noses to shift of the breeze. The clouds of their quick, inquisitive breaths drifted up and away. In the midst of my busy life they reminded me to slow down and just smell the night air.

I tried to smell our runs with them. It starts off with a blast of pine-scented air when we stepped out the front door. Then cut lawns followed by salt-spiced breezes from the bay. We trot along, passing the deep smell of the earth where her vegetative skin of plants had been peeled off to make way for a new subdivision. Then the sour/sweet smell of standing water and wet leaves along the side walk. We pass the gas station with its smells of acrid exhaust and gasoline—for some reason gasoline always smells like pretzels to me. There was a house with a wood-burning furnace or stove whose smell reminded me of camping.

At times, as we ran, the invisible force of a smell was so powerful on my dogs that it would bring our smooth run to an abrupt halt. I assumed these force fields had been deposited by another dog. I was fascinated that they could detect invisible things. It was like running with a couple of metal detectors that would abruptly stop when they had found something. I imagined all the lab tests that I order at work to learn about someone by their urine. I can tell whose urine is infected, who has Chlamydia, who is pregnant, who is starving and burning fat to make ketones, who has liver problems, or kidney problems and spills protein, who is dehydrated, or had a really hard workout. I thought of foods that change the smell of urine and how dogs must have a good sense of each other's diets. I imagine dogs can tell who is in heat, and where those dogs live. What a delightfully gossipy thing to know about your neighbors! Smells are a dog's social media. I imagined my dogs reading these posts with the interest of someone fascinated by the news of others. And sometimes, if they were interesting enough, my dogs would leave their own comments on these threads. As we ran more and more, I wondered if the dogs that would follow us could smell that my dogs ran great distances.

I tried to apply what they taught me. On my bike rides to and from work I learned to recognize and appreciate the smells. There was the restaurant preparing bacon for breakfast, and the diversity of smells of dinner in the houses I passed on my ride home. I can't be sure, but I began to think shady places smell slightly different than sunlit ones. I also experimented with determining—based on the smell alone—if the truck passing me was diesel or gasoline. I had mixed results. I wondered if, with practice, I could determine the type of wood a certain smell of smoke came from.

In our culture we artificially create borders between "civilized" places where we live and "wild" places where nature lives. As I ran with my dogs, this separation fell apart. Wildness and nature surround us. As it fell apart I felt like the story of the proverbial pair of fish who, swimming along see another fish, who asks them, "Hey fellas, how's the water?"

They swim past, thinking about the question, and finally one fish looks at the other and says, "What's water?"

We move through nature, and it can move through us and move our hearts. I just had to be helped to see it. Dogs do that.

The third lesson in their curriculum was that a pack needs a leader. Dogs live in packs, and they make remarkable sacrifices for a pack, because the pack will make sacrifices for its members. In order to survive, the pack must have a leader. Dogs demand leadership, or they will claim it, becoming bossy, hyper, domineering, and almost impossible to live with. A strong follower demands a strong, fair leader, or it will not be a follower for long. They are designed to step up if the leader falls. Dogs respect leaders who have the physical prowess to keep them alive. Dogs are the only animal on earth that will leave members of its own species to be with humans. Part of this is because they recognize that we have the potential to be superb pack leaders.

Leadership depends on establishing expectations. When he arrived at a house with a problem dog Cesar Milan frequently asked, "What behaviors do you want from your dog?" Many times people had not stopped to define and articulate their expectations. But when they were pressed to be specific, often they did have clear, simple, achievable goals: walk without my dog pulling me, or conversely have my dog pull me on rollerblades. For me, I really didn't like it when my dogs pooped on the run because then I had to carry it. Sometimes it would be miles until the next trash can. If I could get my dogs to go poop before our runs, then I wouldn't have to worry about it during the run. Once I had articulated my expectation, I learned that it is possible to teach a dog to go poop before the run. And though it is probably too much information, I adopted this myself, and it proved to be a useful habit on race days...

The converse of leadership is also true: dogs are incredible followers. When corrected for making a mistake, dogs submit their wills with a trusting, pure humility. They are submissive to their pack leader's corrections. When I correct them, my dogs teach me about forgiveness. They watch with careful sideways looks, staying low and waiting to see when they are forgiven. When my body language softens, their own bodies expand, and they come immediately to show me there are no hard feelings: the bond of our friendship would never be hurt by something as small as one of us making a mistake. There is an old joke that asks, "If you leave your wife and your dog in the trunk of your car, after an hour which one will still be happy to see you?"

This relates to the next thing they taught me: celebrate reunions every day. Many days, I would come home from work feeling, in the words of Bilbo Baggins, "like butter that has been scraped over too much bread." My dogs would drop whatever they were doing and greet me at the door with excitement and raw canine joy. They would wag their tails so hard their entire bodies waved hello.

"You came back! Welcome home Master!"

They didn't care if I was late, or if I had been yelled at by my bosses or patients. They didn't care if I had made some humiliating or dangerous mistake. They only cared that I was back. Having me back in the pack was a thing to celebrate. They greeted me with such pure love and adoration that sunlight itself came from the look in their eyes and tried to wash out the gloomy shadows in my mind.

Conversely, dogs have a gentle way of greeting our returns from sleep. Pyper puts her snout right up to my face and with her exquisitely sensitive nose unflinchingly sniffs my embarrassing morning breath. She then gently nudges and licks our faces, which—though annoying—never fails to wake my wife up in a good mood.

Taking them as guide dogs for my poor blind wandering self, I decided that no matter what I was doing, I would work to get up and greet my family members when they came home. And though I forgo the whiffing-of-morning-breath, I decided that the only way to wake a family member is with kisses. My poor teenage son isn't going to know what's coming…

And their final lesson: people have watches, but dogs have time. Dogs measure time differently than we do, because they are actually traveling through their lives at a different speed than we are. They teach us how to be young again, to see the world with wonder:

"What does this stuff taste like? Is that a frog?! Stop everything, what is that incredible smell?"

Then, before our very eyes they teach us how to grow old. Even as we run side by side and stride by stride, my dogs are going faster than me, racing from puppyhood deep into adulthood. Over the course of my semester, which lasted for years of her life, Pyper's muzzle grayed, and she slowed. Paisly went from a bouncing, chewing puppy to a sleek, muscled, and calm adult. Unlike me, they didn't sit around worrying about tomorrow or yesterday. I spend so much time each day fretting over what I need to do the next day, and reminiscing about mistakes or painful conversations that still haunt me. My mind was a time-traveler, always bouncing forward and backward. Dogs learn and move on. Because they trot through time differently, my dogs taught me to live more in the moment because it was the only place our different speeds intersected. They taught me to run the mile I am in. When they look at me, their minds are not elsewhere. They are not dwelling on past hurts, or worrying about the future. They look at me with complete attention, because now is right now.

My love for them is connected to my mind's ability to travel forward and backward in time through the feeling of nostalgia. I mourned them and missed them in the future even when I still have them in the present. I loved my dogs because I knew that with each passing moment I was losing them. As we ran, I wondered if my dogs knew that, like my patients, and my parents, my wife and my residents and everyone that I love, they were running toward their graves. My dogs were blazing past me. And I was hoping I could somehow slow time down by running fast enough, or eating well enough, or studying hard enough, or loving deep enough, or somehow sacrificing great enough. I pulled on their leashes, hoping to somehow slow their aging down.

My dogs smiled and they looked over their furry, gliding shoulders at me, tongues bouncing and tugged back on their leashes: they had one last lesson.

"Watch closely beloved human—who, compared to us, seems to live forever—and we will show you why we run forward with only joy and curiosity in our hearts. We will show you, through our own examples, how to die fearlessly."

No man has the right to be an amateur
in the matter of physical training.
It is a shame for a man to grow old without seeing the beauty and
strength of which he is capable.
Socrates, Philosopher

Somebody may beat me,
but they are going to have to bleed to do it.
Steve Prefontaine, Runner

MILE 11
Second Chances

Metanoia: (Greek) (n) the journey of changing one's mind, heart, self, or way of life.

Like all of my patients, I didn't really have time to exercise. My agenda was thick with events and commitments: I taught a religion class Tuesday nights to college students, mentored my son's boy scout troop on Wednesday nights, attend my children's band performances Thursday and Friday nights, and I didn't train on Sundays. On top of that, I was on-call overnight at the residency program every couple of weeks. But the difference between who I was and who I wanted to be was precisely what I chose to do with my time.

In order to change my life, I had to change my priorities. All of the events I was involved in were important to me. To train for this semester I would have to steal time to exercise. I became a time thief. I stole from my thick, complaining agenda. I stole from my commute. I stole time from watching movies. I stole from surfing the internet. I stole from the time I spent at work. My colleagues seemed mystified that I was leaving early; that I *could* leave early. I had learned that my jobs expanded to fill the time I allowed, and I no longer allowed them to expand so far. I did not steal from sleep, however. I couldn't, I was too tired.

I wanted to steal from my Saturday mornings, but I had given that time to my wife. It belonged to her. I asked her if she was doing anything with it, or if I could have some of it back. She smiled, but did not allow me to steal it. She gave it to me as a gift.

With all of that time, I began training for the first event of the semester: running the 36.8 miles around the bay. Fittingly, this race would be three days before the New Year.

Besides my short, medium and long runs during the week, I had also started riding my bike. It was twelve miles to work, so I rode twenty-four miles on non-running days. I had legitimately addressed each of the doubts that my mind had raised. I found a shower at work. I brought in spare clothes. I bought bike lights and a little backpack for my lunch. Because moths hit my face trying to catch my headlamp, I wore glasses when I rode in the dark. As I found solutions, I discovered my job was actually perfect for training to be an endurance athlete. Most days I sit at a desk for hours. So, instead of feeling guilty about sitting down, I was relieved that I had a job that allowed me to sit and rest from my ride in and prepare for the ride home. I found the time I spent sitting, listening to patients, and working at my desk was transformed. Previously sitting had left me feeling guilty or restless. Now it gave me a feeling of guilty pleasure that I *got to* sit down.

After adjusting to the initial discomfort of resting my weight on my wrists and the narrow bicycle seat, I found I looked forward to the bike days. Biking used different muscles, and actually seemed to rest my tired running legs, while still allowing me to get in more exercise. It felt good to think hard all day while resting my body, and then rest my mind and pedal hard on the ride home. I liked putting my shoes into the stirrup pedals from my father's bike as a gesture of following his footsteps.

As an experiment, I began timing myself to see how quickly I could do the ride. I discovered that I was two to six minutes faster coming home than going to work. When I did get home, I was surprised to discover that I wasn't tired. I actually felt deeply alive. My thoughts had narrowed from their normal flighty, expansive, worrying patterns to a focused, pleasant concentration.

Initially, on mornings when I could see my breath and feel the cold metal of the handlebars through my gloves, I felt intimidating dread. So, like an amateur thermophysiologist, I experimented with the cold. I pushed myself out into the cold and timed how long it would take to warm up. Once I had my data, I could brace against the initial cold shock because I knew it would pass by the time I reached the bridge two miles from my house. The sooner I got there, the sooner I would be warm. I imagined my lungs as two bellows fanning the burn in my quads until they could heat the rest of me enough to stop shivering. Warm, comforting data quieted my waking doubts who claimed the entire ride would be cold and terrible.

"Shhh. The cold will only last two miles."

When I looked at my training chart, I liked what I had created, what I had planned and dreamed. In the third of his seven habits of highly effective people, Steven R. Covey taught that there are always two creations: first mental or spiritual, and then physical. Arnold Schwarzenegger applied this principle to physical endeavors, "It is the mind that creates the body. It is the mind that makes you really workout. It is the mind that visualizes what the body ought to look like as the finished product."

It was interesting to think of the whole semester as a creative act, like it was a piece of art. An act of creation. First I created the semester mentally. Then I trained physically and the which also changed and created my mind. I wondered if that is why it is called "re-creation?" The artist and mathematician Vi Hart once said, "Your greatest creation is yourself. Like any great work of art, creating a great self means putting in hard work, everyday, for years."

Slowly, deliberately, and methodically I formed the habits I would need. Then they returned the compliment and formed me.

As the date for the Around the Bay Relay neared, I learned that after the two of us ran the whole thing by ourselves the year before, Mr. Samac had registered it as an ultramarathon. He had opened it up to other people who wanted to run around the entire bay. Instead of just racing against teams, this year I would actually be competing against legitimate ultramarathon runners. Additionally, two of the stud resident physicians at our program said they had watched me the year before and were going to run the entire thing. They were both younger than me. While I was happy I had inspired them, at the same time I was afraid that they would beat me, along with all the *real* ultramarathoners. I was afraid they would expose me for a false imitation of a real runner, a one hit wonder, a fluke, a fake.

As the training miles accumulated, so did their obstacles and injuries. One resident developed hip pains, the other succumbed to time constrains. Eventually, they told me that they were only going to do part.

On our weekly phone calls, I told my dad about my training. He asked if he could come down. He didn't want to come visit if things were comfortable, but if there was suffering to be had, something difficult to do, then he wanted a part. I could feel his love, and his desire to pour the best of himself into helping me.

On the evening before the run, there was a pre-race meeting for all those who were running the entire course. One of the editors for Runner's World Magazine would be giving a presentation about ultramarathon nutrition. My father came with me. As we pulled up, I noted the number of cars with ultramarathon bumper stickers. Some read "Fifty Miles," some said "Fifty K." Two had Ironman Stickers. The audience of people with chiseled, tan features listened with expressions that appeared both attentive and bored as the editor spoke about carbohydrates and fluid. At the end of her presentation she asked if anyone had any questions about nutrition for endurance events. No one raised a hand. I swallowed, wondering at the collective experience in the room. No one had arrived without considerable training, both with miles and with food. In the eight weeks preceding the race, I had run over twenty miles at a time on my long runs. With each of those I had experimented with nutrition. When no one raised their hand, I assumed everyone else in the room had done the same. Seeing there were no questions, we were told we could start at any time as long as we could finish by one pm.

I laid out my needed supplies in order:

Underwear,

Shorts,
Contact lenses,
Sunscreen,
Reflective belt,
Injinji socks,
Shoes
Chap stick,
GPS watch,
Headlight,
Bananas,
GU gels,
iPod armband,
iPod,
Headphones,
Gatorade,
Salt packets,
Mountain Dew.

I set them all out in a little pile, and tried to go to sleep. I did not sleep well.

The next morning, I got up early. My wife and I drove out to the starting line. I checked in with Mr. Samac and let him know I was starting. He told me that most of the other ultra-runners had left an hour earlier. The relay racers would be starting an hour after me.

I got the dogs out of the van and clicked on my headlight. Starting off, the sea wind was stiff, carrying the smell of ocean and sand. This mixed with the tropical smell of the sunscreen on my face and made the day smell like a vacation. The dogs were excited to be running some place new. They knew that this was our long run day.

My confidence was high. Unlike everyone ahead of me, I had run this course before. This gave my imagination less room to create monsters out of uncertainty and unknowns. I knew where the hills were. I knew where the bathrooms were. I knew I had trained better. I knew what my food plan was. And most importantly, I knew I *could* do it. The first time I ran it, I averaged one mile in ten minutes. This time, my goal was to run nine minute miles.

As we ran, my wife leapfrogged ahead of us every so many miles with our minivan. As the sun rose, I ditched my shirt at one of these meetings to save weight and to once again postpone sweating as long as possible. Managing fluid and hydration is one of the great challenges of endurance events. Eventually the dogs stayed in the van with my wife, and I kept running. The wind was particularly spiteful when I ran across the five mile Mid-Bay Bridge.

As I ran, I thought about all the hours and days of training. When I had first started running, some days I couldn't tell if all this exercise was making me stronger or killing me. To combat my doubts, I had increased the mileage slowly: once I had run sixteen miles, eighteen for the next week was no longer something unimaginable. My mental confidence grew with my physical competence. I thought about the psychological benefit of overtraining. By always running more, I was grateful when my training plan "only" called for thirteen, or twenty six, or thirty miles, whereas before I started training these would have seemed absurd distances.

Much of this psychological training had to do with reference frames. Reference frames shape what we think is both normal and what is possible. Some people believe that running a marathon every Saturday was either excessive or obsessive, but they did not think that sitting on a couch for the same number of hours was abnormal.

As I built the training plan for the semester, I had my previous plan for this race around the bay. But I had no frames of reference for running fifty miles. Looking at training plans for fifty mile ultramarathons, I noticed they all used a marathon training plan as a foundation. Then, they just kept increasing the mileage. One thing they did differently was to back-to-back long runs. The hundred mile training charts all used a fifty mile run to prepare. Like many people, I had thought marathons were as far as humans could run. After all, that distance killed the first recorded man to run it. But here was evidence that human genetic and athletic endurance potential extended even further.

One of the unforeseen perks of my semester was that I recalibrated my reference frames of not only what was humanly possible, but also what was humanly normal. My first reference point was my dad. He had a completely different reference frame for what was normal, and he had built it into me, and my siblings. Because of his example, to this day, all eight of us exercise regularly and are physically fit.

Then, like all children, as I grew I saw my own parents more objectively, and realized the things they did that were unusual. As I saw more overweight and sick patients, I saw how strange and unique my father was.

As the weeks wore on I discovered that, like any good course, my semester had an extensive required reading list. Each of these showed me yet another athlete who found long runs to be normal. Christopher McDougal wrote that we are born to run. In his book, Eat and Run, ultramarathoner Scott Jurek taught that competing helps to keep you eating better. Mishka Shubably wrote in The Long Run, about how ultramarathons helped him fight addictions. In my favorite book on the reading list, Rich Roll's Finding Ultra showed that it was possible to do five Ironman triathlons in five days. In Running on Empty, Marshall

Ulrich wrote about running 3,063 miles in fifty-two days at the age of fifty-seven. To him, it was normal to run over sixty miles a day for almost two months straight. Because such individuals are actually quite rare, I had to surround myself with their thoughts and their stories to counter the other stories of our culture. The stories that led to weakness, obesity, and diabetes.

As I read, I came to believe that running long distances was both quite normal, and completely natural. This was somewhat surprising to me. In changing my reference frames, and changing myself, I was also changing the reference frames of other people. Because they didn't surround themselves with a pantheon of running role models, for some of them I was the only data point they had that humans could do this sort of thing. If a normal, everyday person like me could do this, then it must not be all that impossible.

As the miles increased so did the fatigue. Even though I was catching and passing other runners now, my thoughts soured. I knew they would. I had planned for this. At mile eighteen, I drank a Mountain Dew flavored with GU and a salt packet, put on my headphones and turned on some music. The energy and rhythm of the music drowned out my own thoughts. But I had discovered through experiments that even caffeine and music had a finite half life, so I had another plan for when they stopped working.

My dad wanted to share in the race, but he declined to run it alone. He wanted to run it with me. He was now sixty-three, and had lost some speed so he didn't want to slow me down. After fighting fatigue with music for eight miles, my dad joined me at the marathon point to run the last ten and a half miles. My pace had slowed, and I looked forward to his reviving company.

Just like our marathon years earlier, we ran at a pace compatible with conversation. We jogged along telling stories. A few miles later, my son and daughter also began taking turns running a section with us. They traded off when they reached my wife's next stop. At times we all ran along together, three generations of runners, traveling, talking and teasing. I could hear my father's voice echoing from when I was their age "When you are my age, I expect you to be able to do this. This is the standard." Though they didn't know it, I was happy to be establishing a reference point for them of what was considered normal in our family. There was something nice about three generations all running along together. I was happy they could run with their grandpa.

In his initial response to my announcement of my plan for this semester, my father had warned me about my *other* responsibilities. At the finish line, I met my time goal. I placed third against legitimate ultramarathoners, and more importantly, I also achieved my secret filial and parenting goals.

One day I will find the right words,
and they will be simple.
Jack Kerouac, Poet

Remember that very little is needed to make a happy life.
Marcus Aurelius, Emperor

MILE 12
Aligning Possessions and Passions

Hygge (Danish) (n). A complete absence of anything annoying or emotionally overwhelming; taking pleasure from the presence of gentle, soothing things.

As I ran and rode through January, increasing the miles to prepare for the fifty miler, exhaustion spread from my toes to my teeth. Desperate to refill my emptying enthusiasm tank, I read. I experimented with reading magazines about triathlons or running. However, after flipping through a couple of editions I noticed these magazines left me feeling depleted in a different way. I began craving new shoes, or new running clothes, or a new bicycle. One of the barriers that keeps people from exercising is a pervasive message that tells us that we need the very best stuff in order to exercise, or to have adventures. It suggests that to be a runner you need special running shoes, expensive running shorts, training software, compression stockings, and specially formulated running foods. You must carry water bottles full of specially formulated liquids in your hands when you run, or carry them on a special runner's belt, vest, or backpack. Because it is even more reliant on equipment, biking is an especially easy target. To bike well, the pressure says, you need the lightest carbon fiber bicycle, helmet, and wheels. You need power meters, and your bike must be perfectly fitted to you. The heart of every science experiment is simply counting. So I counted, and the average fitness-type magazine is about thirty-five percent advertisements for equipment, supplements, pills or powders.

I had a friend at work who came into my office one day and looked at my trusty old bike, and said, "Please tell me you aren't going to do the Ironman on that. I just couldn't get comfortable on something like that."

Though there is something pleasant about novelty and progress, believing we need the best equipment before following our dreams can become yet another obstacle that keeps people from trying. As I was making a study of all the barriers, excuses, and voices of doubt that worked on me, I noticed this one was both persuasive and pervasive.

"You can't be a writer until you have a new computer. It'll give you more confidence, and your writing will reflect that."

"You can't be a musician until you have a new instrument. It will sound so much better, and people won't laugh at your old hand-me-down."

"You can't be a photographer until you have a better camera. Your photographs will be so much better. Then you can enter a photo contest. But not with whatever you have now. It just isn't good enough."

"You can't be a romantic man until you have the most recent fashions. Only after you have jettisoned your current fashions will you be beautiful. Only then will you be lovable."

Etcetera. Etcetera, ad nauseam.

The problem with these syllogisms is that they can create a paralysis which keeps us from pursuing our dreams with the stuff we have. If followed to their logical end, the only people running would be the blessed few who have the absolute newest running shoes. The only people writing would be those favored few who have the very latest computers. Music would only be made by the rare chosen individuals with the most expensive instruments. Houses would only be built by builders with the very latest hammers. What a terrible elitist world that would be!

A second problem with nurturing a self-consciousness about the inferior state of our present possessions is that it can lead us to overcompensate. I feel a desperation when chasing transitory trends that tempt me to accumulate more and more. I want new socks, no wait: padded socks! No wait, running socks! The feeling is like one of those movie characters on a crumbling bridge: they are leaping from falling stone to falling stone just fast enough to keep from falling. But as we leap from one pair of falling (yet previously fashionable!) shoes to the next, or from one bike saddle onto the next one, all the ones we have abandoned start to accumulate. All the great myths warn about the dragon who simply sits on a hoard of unused goods and gold. Clutter brings with it its own psychological baggage and stress. There is a Swedish proverb that says, "He who buys what he does not need steals from himself." As I accumulated more and more stuff, I spent more and more time being possessed by my possessions, and less and less time doing the things that brought joy into my life. Luckily the great myths also tell us what we must do about dragons: they must be slain.

So, to give myself psychological breathing room, to allow myself to begin right where my imperfect self and imperfect equipment existed in the present, I pushed back against these arguments. I reassured myself that my value as an athlete was not measured by my stuff. I was trying to collect memories, wisdom, and strength, not stuff. I was trying to make myself more and to have less and less. I embraced the minimalist philosophy of an ascetic.

Ascetic teachers are found in many religious traditions. They led abstemious lives, not always as a rejection of joy, or because self-denial is inherently virtuous, but because it aided their pursuit of inner peace. Though I was not being as severe as some ascetics who lived for months or years in deserts, or gave up all their possessions, I was investing considerable time living a life of greater self-denial than I had ever known. Reading about ancient ascetics gave me more motivation to run than reading magazines about running. There was something familiar about the Greek philosopher Diogenes who used voluntary simplicity (he chose a life of poverty and even lived in a barrel) to criticize the social values of what he saw as a damaged and decadent society. His teachings went on to form the foundation for the Greek philosophy of Stoicism, which taught that self-control and fortitude could make one immune to misfortune. This was the mindset I wanted. Saint Simeon Stylites lived for thirty-seven years on top of a pillar. I imagined people trying to sell him a new pair of shoes or a new robe.

I also studied the minimalists who were a little more contemporary. They each had articulated a response to the market pressure to always seek more:

"There are two ways to get enough: one is to continue to accumulate more and more. The other is to desire less," wrote G.K. Chesterton.

"Teach us to delight in simple things," added Rudyard Kipling.

The great American minimalist Henry Thoreau once said, "I make myself rich by making my wants few."

But perhaps the most influential on me was the modern militant minimalist movement of Dave Bruno's "The 100 Thing Challenge." Bruno conducted a year-long experiment in which he reduced his possessions down to only a hundred things. He found that as each possession was evaluated for inclusion or discard, they forced him to think about what was important to how he wanted to live.

One of the beautiful things about running is that it is an inherently minimalist sport. To participate you really only need four things: shoes, socks, underwear and shorts. Some suggest that you only need underwear and shorts. Some suggest only shorts. And there are a few who would even take issue with that last item. Antoine de Saint-Exupery said, "Perfection is achieved not when there is nothing left to add, but when there is nothing left to remove." Though this applies to many areas of life, I don't believe he wanted people running around in the buff.

I wanted to somehow make more of myself by making less of myself. I wanted to make my life simple and pure. Leonardo da Vinci once said, "Simplicity is the ultimate sophistication." And so I experimented. My preferred running shorts were cotton and cost five dollars at Wal-Mart. McDougal's book Born to Run convinced me to try experimenting with running barefoot. As I ran, I contemplated Thich Nhat Hanh's advice "be aware of the contact between your feet and the earth. Walk as if you are kissing the earth with your feet." Barefoot runners claim that as you run more and more, your soles will reach a balance where the amount of callus formed will equal the amount that is sanded off with each run. One day I saw a female patient who was a barefoot runner, averaging six to ten miles a day. When I examined her feet, they were smooth and free of calluses.

I read about hikers who pushed back against the pressure to buy more and more equipment, the pressure to travel through life with an enormous backpack full of over-engineered gear. These "ultralight" hikers went to extreme lengths to lighten their loads and remove surplus stuff: they cut their toothbrushes down to the head, cut all labels off their equipment, replaced heavy hiking boots with tennis shoes, and then trimmed extraneous shoelaces down to only what was necessary to tie. When they shopped they weighed everything. Sometimes they made their own equipment: they made lightweight stoves from empty cans, they fastened soles of shoes to their feet with twine, and gave up tents in favor of tarps made from shower curtains. Their counter culture solutions were empowering and exciting.

As the semester wore on I thought about how simple my life had become. I was proud my carbon footprint had shrunk. I thought of how little gas I was using to get to work. As I rode my bike, I passed traffic composed of thick people sitting in thick cars sitting in thick traffic. I wondered what it would be like if everyone rode their bicycles. I thought of how biking cut down on pollution, on obesity, *and* on traffic. Then I thought, "Well, these people are not *stuck* in traffic anymore than a tree is *stuck* in a forest. They *are* traffic."

Though I don't believe the elitist view of equipment, I worried I was developing a reverse elitist view and was developing the "pride of the poor." Was I turning into a smug self-righteous bore? Was I going to start evangelizing to people about the purity and righteousness of riding their bikes? "Behold the noble bicycle commuter, carrying the weight of global-warming, obesity, the car drivers and the hope of humanity with the might of his pumping legs."

During this period of minimalism I happened to be studying a course about China. The professor spoke about going to China to teach English back in the nineties, and being amazed at the sheer number of people who rode their bicycles. One of his fellow English teachers was an avid cyclist from Colorado. This teacher told his Chinese students how lucky they were to live in a country that still had so many bikes and hadn't been ruined with cars. His students almost rioted. They were working to make their lives better! They hated their bicycles! There was nothing particularly noble about having to use inferior technology! They wanted cars!

Like that English teacher, I believe in the nobility of simplicity, but acknowledge the painful reality that simplicity has to be voluntary rather than compulsory. True, enriching simplicity is voluntary. Fitness is voluntary. Disciplined study is voluntary. Even human excellence is voluntary.

Not long ago I met a man named Todd Wendel who had through-hiked the entire two thousand plus mile Appalachian Trail. He told me that during his months on the trail, a staple of conversations was hiking equipment. I eagerly asked him if he had met any ultralight hikers. He made a face that told me he was trying to choose his words carefully.

"If you pack heavy then you are uncomfortable when you are carrying everything during the day, but you are really comfortable at night: warm, dry tent, nice sleeping bag, etcetera. If you pack light, then you are comfortable during the day when you are traveling because you aren't carrying much, but you are uncomfortable at night when you are sleeping under a tarp in the rain. You have to pick where you want your hike to hurt."

"So, did you convert and start traveling really light?"

"No. I got annoyed with them to be honest. What difference does it make to anyone else what I am carrying? If I want to carry something heavy it is none of their business. It does not affect them: I am the one who has to carry it!"

I told him about my friend's comment about my old bike, and he laughed knowingly.

During my experiment with running barefoot, I discovered that it did change the way that I ran. I moved much more carefully and softly without shoes because I could feel so much more. Feeling that much more hurt. I found that I had to run on the smoother cement of the sidewalks rather than the coarse asphalt of the street. My feet did harden and callus. However, my calluses did not get worn off as fast as they formed. They grew so thick and inflexible I developed blisters which required removing the entire protective callus to drain. My inexpensive cotton shorts wore out after only a couple hundred miles, exposing my underwear beneath. I imagined my neighbors peering through their blinds with puzzled expressions at me running barefoot and threadbare with my dogs. Rather than feeling enlightened, the path of simplicity left me feeling self-conscious and shabby.

Like the aspiring Chinese motorists, I did not find the lack of technology and the increase in discomfort particularly ennobling. Nevertheless, when I went back to a shoe store I asked for the lightest shoes they had. He showed me two pairs. I tried each pair in turn. Then, I took out an envelope scale, weighed them, and bought the lighter ones. When I arrived home I replaced the shoelaces with shorter, lighter laces. Though it was painful to admit, having new stuff really does give me a jolt of energy, enthusiasm, and confidence.

Secretly I dreamed of buying a new bike, a sleek carbon fiber one that weighed less than my new pair of shoes. I knew I could go much faster on a newer bike. But such a bike would be expensive, and which made me feel guilty. On the other hand, if I followed the path of simplicity and minimalism I found that I felt self-conscious. I could feel guilty or self-conscious. I had to pick which voice of self-doubt I wanted to hear. I was already spending so much time and money on tuition for this semester. Speed costs, and I wasn't sure how fast I wanted to spend. Marie Kondo wrote, "The question of what you want to own is actually the question of how you want to live your life."

Slowly, I traded in my inexpensive cotton socks for Injinji toe socks. Despite lengthy runs, I did not have another blister during the rest of the semester. I discovered it was better to have a few things of high quality than piles of shoddy equipment. I did not buy a new bike. My wife asked me if I wanted one, and said she would support me. I remembered my father's example, and did not feel I had earned a new bike yet.

Life was not always simple when I wanted to live simply. I found it was necessary to let things go: both my possessions, but also my asceticism and smugness, for the simple reason that they were heavy.

We are the recipients of the scientific method.
We can each be a creative and active part of it if we so desire.
It doesn't take a lot of education to check things out.
All it takes is…a minor distrust of everyone else on the planet and
a feeling that they may be trying to put something over on you.
Kary Mullis, Nobel Laureate.

Curiosity will conquer fear even more than bravery will.
James Stevens, Writer

MILE 13
R&D: Experiments with Exercise

Alethiology: (Greek) (n) the study of truth.

Barefoot running and cotton shorts were not my only experiments. Growing up, I read about scientists, these mythical people in lab coats and eye-protecting goggles who paid attention to the world, saw patterns and rules that shaped the world and universe. The Nobel Laureate and physicist Richard Feynman even wrote a book called *The Pleasure of Finding Things Out.*

But as I grew, the joy and awe of figuring things out and having my mind blissfully blown open by a new idea was replaced by the drudgery of memorization and the tension of science fair projects. Throughout medical school we were encouraged to be involved with research and to publish. I felt so excited to not just memorize the known knowledge, but to be invited to actually create new knowledge with science. But publishing in official journals once again became a competitive endeavor filled with tension, judgments, rejections, and a feeling that only the elite were allowed into the club. It didn't feel wonder-filled, or like play. I published a few papers, but felt drained rather than enlivened by the process of discovery.

One year when we went to Sea World. There were multiple animal shows per day, and I wondered when they had time to train these animals. Then I wondered if something else was actually going on. What if the show itself *was* the training? What if the science was happening right before our eyes and we couldn't see it because of the spectacle?

I thought of so many areas of my life where I wish I had more time to practice before I actually had to perform: helping people quit smoking, negotiating with chronic pain patients about their pain medications, giving lectures to the residents, and certainly exercising. What if the practice was happening as I did these things? In some ways a good coach is simply a repository of countless years of experiments. I am both too shy and too cheap to hire a coach, so I decided to use each of my practice runs to methodically research things and check them out for myself. I would try to trick myself into seeing truth the way I have to trick myself to see my own blind spot, or those stars that disappear when you stare straight at them, so you have to approach them sideways…

The idea of discovery just for my own enjoyment felt right again. I imagined myself having a lab book and keeping track of my research results. In no particular order, here are some of my running research results:

Experiment #1: Can I change my running stride to land on my mid-foot instead of heel-striking?

Answer: Yes, but it takes months of running to make this a habit. And on long runs I can only do this for about twenty miles, after that I start heel-striking. And I don't feel bad about it.

Experiment #2: How long would it take for the pain in my lower back, wrists, and backside to stop hurting when I start riding my bicycle to work?

Answer: Two weeks. I just had to hang in there for two weeks of soreness and it went away.

Experiment #3: How many hours can I spend in the sun before I start to get a sunburn?

Answer: Two hours. If I am going to be out longer than that, then I should put on sunscreen.

Experiment #4: If I get a sunburn on one Saturday's long run, will the tan it turns into last until the next Saturday?

Answer: Nope. I'll just get burned all over again.

Experiment #5: How long does eight hour "sport" sunscreen last when running and sweating?

Answer: Four hours

Experiment #6: Is it possible to run a marathon every Saturday?

Answer: Yes, but it means spending all Saturday morning running, eating, and recovering.

Experiment #7: After running a marathon, how much weight do I lose?

Answer: 4lbs.

Experiment #8: Does doing long runs back-to-back on Friday and Saturday teach me anything new?

Answer: Yes, that I hate and dread the second run, but get to practice running when I am already tired.

Experiment #9: How many days does it take me to recover?

Answer: Only one, as long as the next day is only followed by biking.

Experiment #10: Is it possible to run with a full stomach?

Answer: Yes, but it takes about four miles before it settles and my speed is not limited by a thinly veiled threat of gastric rebellion.

Experiment #11: How far can I run before I need a drink?

Answer: It depends on the temperature and how much I sweat. In general, I can run about 8 miles, or an hour or so before I need a drink.

Experiment #12: After really long runs, what does my body crave?

Answer: Not meat. My stomach usually feels so sensitive that I only want fruit smoothies. Even my bones crave cold, liquid, sweet fruity smoothies. With salt. I put salt in them.

Experiment #13: Does cutting out meat change my athletic performance?

Answer: Unclear. From my fairly lean starting weight of 165, I lost about a pound every two weeks for the first couple of months, which may have made me lighter and faster, but mostly I just felt hungrier. I found that I did crave meat, but not before or immediately after exercise. Just later.

Experiment #14: What does cutting out meat do?

Answer: The only thing I can say for certain is that it changes my bowel movements and they don't smell as much. There is something in meat that makes things smell worse.

Experiment #15: When she is actually in shape, how many miles does it take to wear Pyper completely out?

Answer: Even in peak condition, she starts lagging behind me after ten miles and starts to slow me down.

Experiment #16: How many miles does it take to make my dog Paisley tired?

Answer: More than thirty, exact number still undetermined, and will require additional experiments...

Experiment #17: Using my GPS watch, what speeds are my dogs going at each of their gaits?

Answer: Walking is about a fourteen or fifteen minute mile. At my jogging pace of around a ten minute mile my dogs trot. At my running pace of about an eight minute mile my dogs are cantering. And at pace around six minutes per mile my dogs are galloping. Once I learned this, I actually didn't need my GPS watch to check my speed, I could use my dog's gaits to figure out how fast I was going. Also, when my dogs were running, it was like a gear switched in their heads and they didn't stop nearly as often to smell something. Sometimes on walks I was impatient with their stopping and sniffing.

Experiment #18: As mileage increases, what joint starts to hurt first?

Answer: My mid-foot, over the long metatarsal bones of my feet.

Experiment #19: Does exercising this much influence my family to exercise more?

Answer: Some of them. Then again, there may be a really long return on this investment. I didn't start following my father's example until I was in my thirties after all…

Experiment #20: Does stretching help me run faster?

Answer: Nope.

Experiment #21: Does stretching help me not ache as much?

Answer: Nope.

Experiment #22: What the heck does stretching help with?

Answer: Flexibility.

Experiment #23: Do the thick-soled trail-running shoes worn by ultra runners help me run better?

Answer: Nope. Because of the height of their soles, they create a longer lever arm on my ankle joint, which fatigues my ankles.

Experiment #24: Does listening to music affect how far I run?

Answer: Music decreases fatigue. But needs novelty.

Experiment #25: Does music affect how fast I run?

Answer: It depends. Specifically it depends on the beat of the music. If it has a fast beat, *and* either inspiring lyrics or some sort of personal meaning, then it does help me run faster. It seems to do this by distracting my mind from certain tired thoughts that I turned to out of habit.

Experiment #26: Can I use the time I run to study?

Answer: It is pretty much impossible to listen to medical lectures while running. It requires too much concentration.

Experiment #27: So, if I am doing a long run, they always say to run at a pace where you can hold a conversation. Can I run while listening to a book on tape?

Answer: I don't know, I never tried it. But it certainly works while riding my bike, though I use the main speaker instead of headphones as hearing traffic is critical when riding. I did wonder about listening to books on tape while swimming, as it is a fair bit slower maybe it would be more conducive, but I never did buy a swimming iPod or headphones to find out…

Experiment #28: How does my body feel differently when I am running more than fifty miles a week?

Answer: Tired and sore. I think most dedicated athletes must feel this if they are really, really exercising. To be able to exercise constantly requires a high tolerance for constant soreness.

Experiment #29: How tight should I tie my shoelaces?

Answer: Not very tight. Tightness causes more blisters than just having them loose. Once I found the optimal tension, I tied the laces, and never untied them again, preferring simply to slip in and out of the shoes. If I can slip in and out, that's about the right tightness.

Experiment #30: When do I need additional clothing to account for colder temperatures?

Answer: Only shorts are needed if the temperature is over sixty degrees. For fifty to sixty degrees, still no t-shirt is needed, but it takes about a mile before I am warm. A T-shirt is needed for forty to fifty degrees. For thirty to forty degrees: stocking cap and gloves. At twenty to thirty degrees: replace short sleeved t-shirt with long-sleeve, continue stocking cap and gloves. When under forty degrees I was careful to not dress so warmly that I would sweat. It is better to stay cold than to sweat. It isn't cold unless I stopped running and held still. Experiment thirty proved for me the Norwegians aphorism, "There is no such thing as bad weather, only bad clothing."

Experiment #31: What happens if I cut my toenails the night before my long runs?

Answer: The newly exposed skin at the new nail boundaries blisters. Better to cut my toenails *after* a long run and let the skin adapt on the shorter runs.

Experiment #32: How often do I need to cut the dog's nails?

Answer: I don't. As long as I am running with them their nails are filed by the sidewalks and streets.

Experiment #33: After how many miles?

Answer: I don't know, but after the semester began I noticed that their nails had become quiet when they were walking indoors. I suspect that if a dog's nails are audible when they are walking, it might be a sign that their runs are too short. Once they were filed by the miles, my dogs' nails don't touch when they are walking.

Experiment #34: Does having a cold affect my run?

Answer: Nope.

Experiment #35: Do I pedal faster if I replace the bike stirrup pedals from my father with clip-on bike shoes?

Answer: Yes, about two miles an hour faster.

Experiment #36: Am I faster if I buy an aerobar and put that on my bike?

Answer: Yes. Plus it just felt more comfortable to lean onto an aerobar than to put my hands on the low part of the drop bars.

Experiment #37: Can I drink an entire twenty ounce soda before running, or does all the carbonation hurt my stomach and cause cramps, or does the shaking of running make me burp?

Answer: For whatever reasons, it is no problem to drink soda and run. But I feel conflicted about soda, and only use it as a caffeine delivery device on race days.

Like any scientist, not all of my experiments were successes. Like any athlete, neither were all of my runs.

What is the point of being alive
if you don't at least try to do something remarkable?
John Green, Author

I am overwhelmed by the strength of my body and power of my
mind. For one moment, just one second, I feel immortal.
Dianna Nyad, Ultra-endurance Swimmer

MILE 14
Running Fifty Miles

Alamort: (French) (adj) half dead of exhaustion.

On my father's sixty-fourth birthday I ran fifty miles.

As usual, the night before the race, I didn't sleep well. The more I wanted sleep, the more irritated and filled with dread I became when I wasn't able to. And so I became anxious about feeling too anxious and afraid of getting adrenaline from being afraid. But after already experimenting with insomnia on the run around the bay I learned that if I didn't sleep well before a race, it didn't really matter. Insomnia was just the first challenge of any race, the first obstacle to be overcome, the first doubt to be silenced. After using the first race of the semester as an experiment, I knew that it had no detectable effect on my performance. I also hoped by learning this and really accepting it would stop me from worrying at the next event so I could sleep.

In my pockets I carried two baggies of exactly four wipes each, but thanks to adrenaline's effect and following my dog's example, I didn't know if I would need them. I assembled my usual equipment. I made sure the shorts I was wearing didn't have any obvious holes.

Because I had never run something this long before, I had to rely on the experience of others. I found and followed a fifty-mile ultramarathon training chart available on the Internet. It had a three week taper, to allow a runner to heal-up prior to such a long run. I didn't know what to do about that: I only had seven weeks from the time I ran around the bay. I worried that if the taper was too long I would, instead of resting and healing-up, actually decondition. Prior to my thirty-six mile run I had only tapered one week. I kept faith with the authors of the plan, but decided to test their hypothesis for myself and find out.

The people at this event were a completely different species of human beings. I felt like an anthropologist studying an elusive tribe, or a secret society that disperses and lives undetectably among normal people, only to congregate in detectable numbers at ultramarathons. There was one guy who had had both of his knees replaced. Another was deaf, and there was a woman who appeared to have cerebral palsy. The event was actually three different runs, a fifty-mile, a hundred km (or sixty-two mile), and a hundred mile. The distance depended on how many laps were completed.

There was an atmosphere of loneliness as everyone set out together. Perhaps this was why they were the most welcoming athletes I had ever met. Striking up conversations with fellow runners was expected and even encouraged. Though membership in the tribe was offered freely, there was no easy way in. Membership dues were paid with miles, pain tolerance, and a willingness to run really, really far.

The tribe revered its elders. Several of the older runners had long gray or white beards. Following the custom of striking up conversations, I strode alongside a gentleman with a gray beard and an unhurried pace and started asking him questions. I learned he had been running since the 70's (not continuously, but pretty close). He told me he used to race and had won some ultras. He had set some course records, then coached some, but now he just ran for fun. He said he tried to do a hundred miler every three months or so. He knew most of the runners around us, and they all said hello as homage to him as they came by.

"After we lose our agility, speed, and strength, endurance is the last athletic feature to go. I'm going to enjoy it while it lasts."

He had some friends who had stopped doing hundred mile runs in their seventies, and then just ran fifty milers, and then back to marathons, then back to ten Ks.

I asked about what he thought of shoes. He quietly admitted that he was actually a shoe tester for one of the big shoe companies. They sent him new shoes they were developing and he would run in them for a couple of weeks. He'd provide feedback after each run, and then they'd send him another pair after about 160 miles. I asked, after all that experimenting and research, which ones he liked best. He told me that when he wasn't testing, he ran in the same brand of shoes he always had for the past twenty-two years.

I asked him about his diet and what he ate. He said that he used to have special meals when he was racing. But now he was doing this for fun, so he ate whatever his wife happened to have prepared the night before.

It seemed like he was telling me something about shoes and food but I couldn't quite understand. I felt like my questions were missing the point somehow. He reminded me of an old wizard who had given me a riddle I couldn't yet solve.

Another of these old graybeards made me think he was using magic. I passed him four different times during the first fourteen miles, without ever seeing him pass me. Each time I caught him he was walking. It made me feel like I was running backward. The fourth time I asked him what he was doing. He explained that he used a ratio. He ran for seven minutes, and then walked for three minutes. I learned that many people were trying to maintain a run to walk ratio. Some ran eight minutes (or miles), then walked two. Some ran five miles (or minutes) and then walked one. Though I hadn't thought of it in those terms, I realized I had iterated into a similar strategy. At my last race, I had been able to run thirty miles before I needed to walk, so I thought I would try to run ten miles, and then walk one, and repeat this five times. Because I had run the thirty-six mile run in six hours I reasoned that it would probably take me another three, maybe four hours to run the additional fourteen miles to reach fifty. I estimated I would run this fifty miler in ten hours at the most.

Before he passed me for good around mile thirty-four I asked him if having a beard was warm. He said it was not. I wondered if there was some sort of primordial benefit, so I asked if it helped hold moisture and helped cool him down. He said it did not, then laughed and said "All it really does is get in the way when I'm eating!"

I'd never wanted a beard until I met these guys; they just looked so primal and wild. They were literally the same guys who were running back during the running craze of the '70s that had caught my father and others of that generation. A part of the movie *Forrest Gump* referenced this craze when he starts running across the country, but these guys were the real thing, and they were still running. Some of those guys are still out there. They looked the way my imaginary running caveman ancestors looked, all bearded and wiry and fluid. It was impossible not to respect a seventy-year-old guy who could outrun me.

As we ran along, a common greeting was to ask each other which of the three distances we were running. Because I couldn't tell which distance anyone else was running I assumed they were all running farther than me. When I was asked about my goal, I sheepishly admitted that I was *just* running the fifty miler.

I was laughed at.

But not because of the distance, because of my qualifier.

"There is no *just* distance," one friendly runner and his partner corrected me.

"There is no *just* a mile. There is no *just* a half marathon. No such thing as *just* a fifty miler."

"Hey, if you worked and trained hard enough to get here and run fifty miles then you are allowed to claim it and be proud of it."

"Yeah," added his friend, "you can be a badass and humble at the same time."

"Not that he knows what either of those feels like," teased the first runner.

Only the top few folks in each run were competing with each other in a race. There were extra awards for the top finishers of each race. Instead of reverence, the tribe accepted the racers with the same easy equanimity. It was just accepted that some people's demons and dreams whipped them to race. All the rest of us had our own fears and goals riding us like jockeys. There were no gender differences, no age differences. Pain leveled and equalized us all. They are the only competitors I have ever met who understood they were really just competing with themselves.

After the first ten miles, I felt good. The day was beautiful, and the vibe of this tribe was so energetic. I figured I'd just run another ten miles, and then start with my planned ratio. I saw people around me walking, and rather than learning from their experience and humility, I went for the short term buzz of passing them. I hadn't yet learned to domesticate my competitive heart.

Around mile twelve I caught up with one of my wife's friends named Des. Des had been running ultras for some time, and knew many of the people around us and met even more of them as we ran. She was a wealth of running lore about both the physical and the mental terrain. Privately I thought of her as Sacajawea. As we started talking I came to realize that like all the great ultra-runners I had read about, Des too had a demon she was running from. She mentioned that her husband was in jail. She didn't elaborate, except to say that if he ever tried to run after her, she would run even further. She had a wildness to her that was completely fascinating, and completely mysterious.

The race course had a unique shape. It went out and back down three long paths, like the spokes of the Mercedes-Benz symbol, through six foot shrubs and Saw Palmetto groves. Because of this we were always passing other runners going the opposite direction on the same trails. Because few were really competing in the usual sense, it was customary to offer words of encouragement when approaching someone going the other way. Des and I experimented with various catch phrases, such as "Hey," and "Hey, hey." I thought "Looking strong," was nice. Des complimented various items of their outfits, or said, "Nice legs," a phrase I imagine most runners appreciated, but that I didn't think I could get away with.

After hours and many iterations, we finally decided our favorite was, "You got this." This phrase left it open to their own subjective interpretation as to what exactly "this" was. It could be whatever they were aiming for at that particular moment: "this" mile, "this" stretch of woods, even "this" bathroom break.

Enjoying the conversation, I also ran past twenty miles.

Because this was a trail run, about seventy-five percent of it was on sandy paths. I lost count of the number of times I stopped to empty my shoes and brush off the soles of my socks. By mile forty, as my legs stiffened up, it became pretty much impossible to bend over to get my shoes off. I noticed that some runners did not have this problem because they wore cute, tight little running gaiters over their shoes to keep the sand out. I asked about them, and they swore by them, saying they never had to shake out their shoes, nor did the elastic around their ankles chafe. This was one piece of equipment I wish I had field tested.

One thing I *had* field tested that puzzled me immensely were the water bottles everyone carried. I had already figured out that in these temperatures I didn't need to drink except every hour or so. The aid stations were roughly every seven miles. I didn't understand why anyone would want to carry an extra two pounds in each hand. Alternatively, many runners had hip belts for their water bottles, or running vests/backpacks. These were all quite interesting, but depending on how much fluid was in them, they weighed between one and five pounds. I just couldn't imagine running any significant distance with dumbbells in my hands, or a weight vest on. I preferred to carry my water and food in my stomach where, besides being over my center of gravity, it was being put to immediate use. Otherwise I was content to just let it sit on the aid station tables.

Because they were seven miles apart, I ate at every aid station. They had chairs to rest in, and people who were cheering and saying flattering things about us.

"You guys are awesome!"

"What do you need?"

Like a good guide to a naïve adventurer, Des warned me that aid stations were like the island of the Lotus-eaters mentioned by Odysseus in The Odyssey:

"Here we landed to take in fresh water, and our crews got their mid-day meal on the shore near the ships. When they had eaten and drunk I sent two of my company to see what manner of men the people of the place might be... They started at once, and went about among the Lotus-eaters, who did them no hurt, but gave them to eat of the lotus, which was so delicious that those who ate of it left off caring about home, and did not even want to go back and say what had happened to them, but were for staying and munching lotus with the Lotus-eaters without thinking further of their return; nevertheless, though they wept bitterly I forced them back to the ships and made them fast under the benches. Then I told the rest to go on board at once, lest any of them should taste of the lotus and leave off wanting to get home, so they took their places and smote the grey sea with their oars."

I wanted to stop, to sit in the chairs for just a minute. Some supporters were rubbing the runner's shoulders! Some were offering free foot rubs! Des told me to just pick up food and keep walking. I picked up banana halves, stacks of Pringles, and (at least) two drink cups each time. I carried the food and walked away from the inviting chairs.

When I ran past thirty-seven miles it was the farthest I had ever run, and I was in completely uncharted territory. I did not know how my body would respond, or behave. I learned the hard way. Somewhere around this point I lost my guide Des. She had returned to the woods from whence she came. I was alone. I turned on my iPod to try to draw strength from music.

As the miles increased the percent of time I spent walking and the percent I spent running slowly reversed until at mile forty-two I couldn't run. This was both disorienting and terrifying. I felt vulnerable. If something came out of the woods to attack me, I could no longer run away. If I got hurt I could not run for help. I worried that my ability to walk would also start to crumble, and I would become completely immobile.

Those who had paced themselves and stuck to their run to walk ratios passed me. When I could no longer run, I suffered the consequences of not sticking with my original plan to run ten miles and then walk one. I learned that it takes more discipline to slow down than it does to speed up. At these distances, in order to go fast it is necessary to go slow. I did not give myself a chance to run my own run.

One of the reasons I had entered this race was I wanted to find the physical limitations and boundaries of my own body, of my own motivation and of myself. What I was not expecting was that those boundaries blur into other people. Humans are not solids, we are permeable. When I was exhausted I did not draw strength from myself, I drew it from others. The friendliness, encouragement and stories of the other runners reached through my boundaries. Because we are porous creatures, some runners were strategic about having people from whom they could draw encouragement late in the race. They had pacers.

I didn't have a pacer, but I drew strength from my father; from the fact he called my wife to check on me in the middle of the race, on his own birthday. I drew strength from the fact that he remembered me and was cheering for me. He asked my wife about my times and how I was eating, and how I looked. I drew strength from Katie and the light in her eyes each time I saw her at an aid station. I drew strength from my kids, and from wanting to leave them with a legacy and example as my father had before me. I drew strength from the fact that my son was running a 5k that morning with his friends, and my daughter was in her first one mile fun run. At one of the stops, Katie told me that at eleven years old our daughter had run the mile in 5:58. I drew strength from how proud I was of her. I drew strength from the workers at the aid stations. I drew strength from my primal ancestors who ran to survive. I drew strength from my dogs, with whom I had run countless hours preparing for this race. At mile thirty-nine the song "Gone, Gone, Gone" by Phillip Phillips came on.

When you fall like a statue,
I'm goin' be there to catch you.
Put you on your feet, you on your feet.
And if your well is empty,
Not a thing will prevent me.
Tell me what you need, what do you need?

I found strength to run a little more as I imagined my dogs and how much they would love a run in the woods like this. I imagined Paisly lying on the floor of our house, running in her sleep, dreaming of running with me. I imagined her catching me in her dream, looking up at me, smiling her perfect canine smile, and willing me to keep going.

You're my back bone.
You're my cornerstone.
You're my crutch when my legs stop moving.
You're my head start.
You're my rugged heart.
You're the pulse that I've always needed.
Like a drum, baby, don't stop beating.
Like a drum baby, don't stop beating.
Like a drum baby don't stop beating.

At mile forty-three, my mind began folding in on itself.

The music I was listening to stopped working to motivate my steps to match the beat.

It became more difficult to offer words of encouragement. As my own courage diminished, I had less to give to others. On the last mile, it was all I could do to grimace out a smile and wave as I lost the desire and ability to form coherent words. Many of the runners stopped making eye contact as they receded inside their own minds. Their eyes looked like those of a hunted animal.

The only time one of the members of this tribe said something that approached reproach was around mile forty-five. As I shuffled by another runner I tried the universal human conversation starter: sharing what I thought would be a common complaint. I mentioned that I was in more pain that I had ever felt.

"Do not think that way," I was told.

Whining was not accepted by this tribe.

As I tried to get comfortable with being uncomfortable, I found my awareness of my surroundings decreased, but my awareness of pain increased until I was the most uncomfortable I have ever felt in my life. Strangely, and unlike most of the patients I have seen who claim to have a 10/10 pain, I also became more aware of kindness. When I went through the last aid station, the concern and alertness of the aid workers brought tears to my eyes. Through soft sobs I thanked them for being there and supporting us.

Katie was there. I asked her to help me get the sand out of my socks and shoes one last time as I could not bend over to get my shoes off any more. When her warm, energetic hand touched my sore and painful feet, I started crying again. She reminded me of a poem by Anita Krizzan, "If you feel like you are falling apart, fall apart into my arms. I promise I will catch every little piece of you and I promise I will love your brokenness."

As the pain increased, I began to pray. I hadn't wanted to bother Him, but I felt hope leaving me. My prayer was simple:

"Dear God, I am alone. I hurt. Please run with me for a little ways. Dear God, I am alone and I hurt, please run for me a little ways."

Interestingly this actually helped quite a bit and I was able to run again for a little while. When I could no longer run, rather than feeling abandoned, I thanked Him for the help. I imagined God smiling at me and saying it had been fun to run with me, and thanking me for the invitation, and saying we should do it again sometime. In my mind I asked Him if He was pleased with me. When I opened my eyes from this little prayer, my eyes were greeted with a beautiful smoothie-colored sunset.

I had run and walked from sunrise to sunset, for eleven straight hours. My wrist GPS was warning that its battery life was ending just as my own internal physical and emotional batteries warned the same thing. Near the finish line were some of the Tribal Elders who were not running this time. Among these old bearded ultra-runners was one who still held a course record for a crazy ultramarathon down in Brazil. I had seen them earlier; people had been getting their autographs. They stood up from their lawn chairs and clapped for me as I approached the finish line. It was like having my childhood heroes show up to clap for me, instead of the other way around. I cried to have earned their applause and to have actually accomplished something this big.

Crossing the finish, I hit stop on my GPS watch. It read, "51 miles, 11:04."

As I left, I thanked the race director for putting the race together. Night was falling. I sat on the back bumper of our van and looked at the runners who were still going. All of us who were doing the fifty miler were finishing, leaving only the strong. Des, who had run with me for hours, still had twelve more miles in the darkness to complete her hundred kilometers. My mind could not wrap around the idea of running through the night, I was already a zombie. I looked at the runners who were doing the full hundred miler. They were only halfway, and that was the easy half! The daytime half, the half with all the company and energy of the rest of us. I saw them shuffle by and felt a level of awe that bordered on fear. I had run alongside them all day, pretending I was one of them, but now, in the darkness I could see them for who they really were: gods and wizards and the undead. As I crawled into my sleeping bag in the back of our van, I felt like I was dying, and being carried away in the back of a hearse. I was glad to be done, glad to be able to flee that place and those terrifyingly possessed people.

And yet, as we pulled away, and I considered what I had just done, I never felt so alive. It was a deeply satisfying feeling to do something that I had once believed impossible.

If you keep good food in your fridge,
you will eat good food.
Errick McAdams, Athletic Trainer

It is very, very important for your dog's psychological health,
his whole entire being—if you want to call it his "soul"—
that he <u>earn</u> the food he receives.
Cesar Milan, Dog Whisperer

MILE 15
Stay Hungry

Slake: (n) to allay (thirst, desire, wrath, etc.) by satisfying.

Once upon a time, I had a patient whose weight was causing health problems.

I asked about diet and exercise.

"I only eat salads and baked chicken, and I go to the gym for an hour a day and I still can't lose weight."

I could feel the patient's discouragement, desperation, defensiveness, and even despair. Over the years as a physician I had had iteration after iteration of this conversation. Though I had gained weight during medical school, it had not been difficult to lose once I simply started moving. But the durability and redundancy of this conversation with patients left me curious about how difficult weight loss below my body's seemingly fixed weight actually was.

Like most people, I frequently feel confused with food. Despite years of education on nutrition, I don't always know what I'm doing when I am reading food labels. On the days when I didn't run with my dogs I felt guilty, like I let them down. So I would give them treats to try to make it up to them, to soothe my own guilt. Like many things about our relationship, it was symbolic of my relationship with myself. And sometimes, in an act of benevolent selflessness, I ate all of the junk food in the house in the name of protecting my family.

Thirty percent of Americans have a body mass index (BMI) over twenty five and are therefore overweight. Another thirty percent have a BMI over thirty and are therefore obese. Innumerable patients ask their physicians for help with weight loss. Many of these patients develop weight-related diseases, and their relationships with food become even more tangled. Wanting to be helpful as a physician I read self-help books, diet books, medical textbooks and journal articles trying to find things that would help them. Though I didn't start the semester wanting to learn anything new or specific about nutrition, my training directly affected my relationship with food. And so, I added another area of study to my semester of experiments: nutrition.

I experimented on myself with weight loss.

I found that every food choice became more nuanced as I considered how that particular food would affect either my recovery from my last run, my current run, my next run, or my next race. At the end of each long run I tried to listen to my joints for aches, my muscles for soreness, my skin for chaffing, and my gut for cravings or aversions. I imagined my gut as a big energy extraction plant, into one end food was shoveled. As it flowed through sweaty pipes it was divided and sorted and shiny energy was extracted along with blasts of steam. The energy was then fed into the furnaces of my legs and fanned by the bellows of my lungs. What kind of food did this system want me to put into it?

When I began, I had no sense of scale, of how many calories I was burning, nor of how many I was replacing with my food. I had heard of people who counted calories, but it seemed unbearably tedious. I imagined the act of counting calories sucked both the flavor and joy out of the food. Basically after exercising I was hungry and so I ate. A lot. I began to understand why people could go to the gym and exercise for "an hour," and not lose weight. They could replace all those calories quite easily.

One of the reasons it is so difficult to lose weight through exercise stems from the fact that humans are designed to be incredibly efficient athletes. Depending on weight, and how fast we are running, humans burn roughly a hundred calories to run one mile (it is actually closer to 125 calories per mile for men and 105 for women but I like to keep the math simple). One hundred calories is two and a half Oreo cookies. And who eats half an Oreo cookie? Our bodies are such efficient machines that our mouths can write checks our bodies can't cash.

During the fifty-mile run, aid stations were roughly seven miles apart. Instead of thinking of them as miles apart, I began to think of them as seven hundred calories apart. Ideally, I would just replace all those calories at each aid station. A banana is about a hundred calories, so that would require eating seven bananas at each aid station. In my experiments I had found it was possible to eat an entire banana before running, without getting cramps, but seven seemed like I would be pushing it.

Prior to this race, I had never "hit the wall." I had heard about it, but never felt it. It felt horrible. This phenomenon is caused by completely running out of stored sugary carbohydrate fuel. To keep our blood sugar from swinging wildly high after meals and crashing dangerously low in-between meals, the body stores sugar in the muscles and liver in a branched molecule called glycogen. When sugar is needed, the body taps into this energy reservoir and carefully breaks glycogen back down during times of drought. Most humans have enough glycogen storage to last around twenty-four to thirty-six hours of fasting. When running, we usually only have enough of this type of fuel for about twenty miles. This is where marathoners speak about "bonking" or "hitting the wall." Though they can burn fat, muscles prefer to burn sugar. The brain only uses sugar; it cannot use fat, though it will reluctantly use a fat-burning by-product called a ketone.

When my body was all out of carbohydrate and my brain had to be fueled on ketones, I could feel its effect on my thought content and mood. I started to think grumpy, angry thoughts about people, and about the world. I started to relive old arguments, and have "stinking thinking." It was interesting that anger would be the emotion my body was designed to preserve for this low mental state. It must serve some valuable purpose, but it remains a mystery to me. I did have to learn to recognize that my grumpiness and negative thoughts frequently represented carbohydrate deficiency. Curiously, my wife was more sensitive to my moods than I was, and she frequently told me to eat before I even felt hungry.

An athlete's ability to replace carbohydrate calories is one of the deciding factors before they "hit the wall." One way around this wall is to train our bodies to use fat by regularly running distances around twenty-miles. Leading up to the fifty miler, I did my long runs, but sometimes under the schedule constraints of my family's Saturday activities, I had to break them up into chunks that were smaller than twenty miles, and ate in-between which replaced the missing carbs instead of letting my body practice burning fats. So I never really "bonked" completely in practice. This principle was why the smart runners had paced themselves with their alternating walk and run cycles. This allowed their bodies to aerobically convert lactic acid back into glucose through a biochemical process called, "the Cori Cycle."

If I was going to do even longer events, I realized I would have to spend more time experimenting with food.

Even the leanest human has plenty of fat to run incredible distances. When I began the semester I weighed 165 pounds. Assuming six or seven percent body fat (I never had it measured), that is ten to twelve pounds of fat. Now, here's where things get interesting. As mentioned earlier, it takes about a hundred calories to run a mile. There are three thousand calories in a pound of fat. So if we are efficiently using it as fuel, one pound of fat allows us to run thirty miles! Assuming I could burn all of it without dying, my ten to twelve pounds of fat could have allowed me to run between 300 and 360 miles! Fat is just untapped potential energy. Some people just have more untapped potential than others.

I found that I was losing about two pounds per month with all this exercise. But there is a catch: to lose weight more calories must be burned through exercise than the gut absorbs through eating. To lose one pound by running requires adding nothing new to the diet, and running an additional thirty miles! As the saying goes, you can lose ounces in the gym, and pounds in the kitchen. My experiments confirmed: weight loss through exercise is possible, but it oversimplifies the complex relationship we each have with food.

Over the course of the semester my relationship with food slowly changed. Instead of just eating out of boredom or guilt, I started to feel differently about food. I began to feel like I was allowed to eat. Then, I started feeling like not only was I *allowed* to eat, but that I had actually earned my food. Then I began feeling like I *had* to eat to make it through the next day's run. Even when I wasn't hungry, I forced myself to eat.

I did numerous other experiments with food. After all, I wasn't really trying to lose weight; I was trying to optimize my performance. My next events would require me to experiment with riding more on my bike, and swimming as well.

I experimented with logging my foods in various apps. I wondered how many calories I could eat while riding on the bike.

I experimented with the glycemic index of foods. This number represents how quickly a food can be converted into glucose. Low glycemic index foods are converted more slowly, giving a steady amount of sugar over a longer period of time. High glycemic index foods are converted to glucose quickly.

I experimented with sugary "performance" gels that promised to refill my depleting glycogen stores. Most of these had a pretty high glycemic index. I found that Hammer gels, which came in packages shaped like hammers, required two hands to open and squeeze, leaving my hands messy and sticking to my handlebars when I was riding. I preferred GU gels, and put them in my Gatorade along with salt. By the end of most races I was sick to my stomach of eating sweet things. I learned about a less sweetened product called HEED that my palate tolerated better than Gatorade.

I experimented with hydration. This one is easy to over think. Basically, my rule was: take liquids at every aid station. If I wasn't thirsty, I took water. Rather than risk diluting my blood salts to get it to my sweat glands, I just poured the water on my head to cool myself off directly because, hey, much of it was heading for my skin via sweat glands anyway.

After reading Scott Jurek's book, Rich Roll's book, watching Michael Arnstein the fruitarian's ultramarathon videos on YouTube, and watching the documentary <u>Forks over Knives</u>, I experimented with being vegetarian. Though I was an imperfect vegetarian the result of those particular experiments taught me primarily that eating veggies the afternoon before races helped me poop. This wasn't a bad thing, and probably even more important for some vegetarians who frequently seemed a bit, er, stuck. As omnivores, our digestive tracts are the gastronomic equivalent of the multi-sport athlete. We are culinary cross-trainers, and though I love running, if someone tells me that it is the only, or the best sport, I tell them to go eat vegetables. I believe we need a diversity of foods, including meat.

Interestingly, in 2013 Axelsson et al. published findings in the journal Nature that showed that one of the key genetic differences between dogs and wolves involves genes that allow domestic dogs to digest carbohydrates. Instead of being obligate carnivores like wolves, they became omnivores, like us. This increased our symbiosis.

Though I love experimenting, there is something about the "scientific simplification" approach that misses an important point: nutrition is greater than the sum of its parts.

Against my original intentions, I was attracted to family medicine as a specialty precisely because of its omnivorous approach to the diversity of problems it addressed. My heroes were frequently polymaths rather than specialists; mental omnivores whose interests ranged widely like Michaelangelo who once said, "God grant me that I may always desire to do more than I can accomplish." To keep my mind balanced, I found that I needed a diversity of interests. My success at one area of my life helped to buffer me against set-backs, criticisms, and doubts in another area. The problem with specializing mentally, or gastronomically is that it involves learning more and more about less and less until you know absolutely everything about basically nothing. I wanted to learn about *everything*. I wanted to taste and experience everything.

When I was in Korea, my Korean friends and I loved to discuss the differences between our cultures. One of them, Ms. Yun, told me about how puzzling it was to her that her American friend, who was training for some ultras, used special ordered electrolyte replacement drinks. I had just watched the Discovery Channel series about climbing Mount Everest. In it, the American climber Tim Medvetz explained that before pushing on to the summit he was eating a gel packet of specially formulated electrolytes, carbohydrates, micronutrients and vitamins he had ordered for just this day.

Russell Brice, the guide from New Zealand, overhears Medvetz, and says, "Well I'm eating a boiled egg. And that is the difference between Americans and the rest of the world: the rest of us still eat real food."

I see so many patients who over think and try to over-engineer their consumption of water. They think they need to drink eight glasses of water a day. Some carry around gallon sized jugs that they try to force themselves to drink each day. After admitting several of these folks to the hospital for hyponatremia I tell them to just relax, and trust the thirst sensors that our ancestors built into our bodies. They argue that they read they should do this based on "science."

Ms. Yun asked me if I am comfortable sleeping on the floor. I admitted that it usually takes me a few nights to get used to it. I had seen the austere Korean beds at a furniture store: they were slabs of heat-able marble or stone. She said she can sleep on a mattress, but that she is just as comfortable sleeping on a hard floor. The Spartan part of me found that incredibly admirable.

"But my American friends cannot sleep on the floor because it is too uncomfortable," said Ms. Yun. She then added, "It is confusing. I sleep because I am tired, not because of a mattress."

On another occasion, a friend from Hong Kong and I went to the supermarket to buy some snacks for a party. As we passed the medication aisle she grabbed my arm and stopped us. Pointing down the aisle she asked me, "Travis, why do white people take so much medicine? Do you get sick easily?" I laughed, having never considered a medicine aisle to be an unusual feature of a supermarket. Medicine and food have had a long and complex relationship since ancient times.

So, there was one final lesson about food. It is probably best illustrated by another patient I saw some years ago.

She was barely five feet tall, and was pushing 350 pounds. Her weight was causing her knee pain I think.

Personally I had given up on suggesting diet and exercise, replacing them instead with "eat and train." This created an important psychological shift. I didn't think she was ready for that shift yet. I asked her what she thought were her biggest barriers to weight loss.

She took a deep, slightly panicked breath. "My husband isn't supportive," she began "The gym doesn't have exercise classes I'm interested in."

"And food?" I asked.

"The recipes in diet books aren't foods that I even like," she replied "And my doctors never tell me what I am supposed to do. They have never told me which diet pills to take."

In the discipline of psychology's terms, this is called having an "external locus of control." It was an elegantly orchestrated psychological escape attempt from the heavy burden of responsibility. However, the charitable donation of responsibility for her weight problem to external factors over which she had no control (her husband, the gym, diet books, and me her physician) had also given away her power to control it and left her with a different kind of heaviness.

When we look to food as the solution for our fitness, we shift to an external locus of control, and it risks weakening us. People have done every sport on earth fueled by things ranging from broccoli to bourbon. When we look to running shoes as the solution for our running, we shift to an external locus of control and risk weakening ourselves, blaming them for our suboptimal performances or injuries so now we are no longer responsible. When we look to our mattresses for sleep, our bikes for speed, diet pills for weight loss, or our medicines for our health we risk withering mentally.

During the fifty-miler, when I asked that old guy about his shoes and his diet, he hinted that I was missing the point. I was trying to shift responsibility for his seemingly super-human running to external things. He refused to be weakened in that way. He ran because he was a runner, and runners run, period.

I survived because the fire inside me
burned brighter than the fire around me.
Joshua Graham, Burn Victim

It's supposed to be hard.
If it wasn't hard, everyone would do it.
The hard is what makes it great.
Jimmy Dugan, Athlete

MILE 16
Changing Gears

Numinous: (Latin) (adj) describing an experience that makes you fearful yet fascinated, awed yet attracted—the powerful, personal feeling of being overwhelmed and inspired.

For the third race of my semester, I switched from being a pure runner to being an athletic omnivore, a triathlete. I would do three different events in a half ironman triathlon. Because it was not Ironman brand, the correct term was "half" which made it seem much shorter than it actually was. It would be a 1.2 mile swim, followed by a 56 mile bike ride, and then a 13.1 mile half marathon. I had to change my training so it included more cycling, and I find a way to train for the swim.

As my bike ride to work was only twelve miles, and then twelve miles back home, I needed a way to increase my bike mileage. Once again I heard familiar, grating voices clearing their phlegmy throats as they approached.

"We couldn't help but notice that every time you ride your bike to work you have a close encounter with a car. Have you so little misery in your life that you must create more?"

"How are you still here? I just ran fifty miles trying to get away from you!"

"Anyway, we've been doing our own little science experiment. It's called, 'how often does he almost get hit by a car?' So we've been counting, and it looks like you have roughly one risky encounter per hour."

"I haven't been hit."

"Yet. You see, if you increase your practice rides to fifty miles, you're gonna hafta ride two and a half to three hours to get in some fifty mile practice rides, so that increases your odds of getting hit by a hundred percent! Good luck with that."

"You think it will break your leg when the car smashes into the side of your bike, or do you think you'll break your arm when you fall onto that skinny little twig going twenty five miles an hour?"

"I've been losing weight on purpose. I'm lighter and faster."

"Aren't you bored with the sheer monotony of all this? Haven't you done enough already to prove your point?"

"I'm going to finish this."

"Ok, just one more thing. Enjoy spending even more time away from my family…"

Was this why it was so hard for my patients to exercise? These voices were exhausting! Listening to them was a whole other endurance sport. Maybe this wasn't going to be just three events; I still had to overcome these pernicious voices of doubt. But they were just another obstacle to be overcome. I wasn't trying to limit my challenges; I was trying to challenge my limits.

One of the residents at the hospital told me about a road near the hospital on a private government road, so the car traffic was tightly controlled. Consequently the local biking clubs all got special passes to ride their bikes on these roads to avoid traffic. According to my GPS, from my house to the far end of the road was exactly twenty-five miles.

The second solution I found in an article on a triathlon website. The author wrote that most professional triathletes rode their bikes indoors to avoid the risk of being hit. A few days later, on what appeared to be a chance encounter, my wife and I were in a department store. In the sporting goods department there was a stationary spin bicycle on sale. It was the last one in stock—the floor model—and had been sharply discounted. Normally this model was selling for five hundred dollars. We bought it for two hundred. I filed this expense not under "tuition," or "books," but rather as "lab fees."

I set it up in our living room, and solved several problems at once: how to get in more biking miles without any more risk of being hit?

"Check."

How to spend more time with my family?

"Check."

How to break up the monotony of training?

"Check."

Even at full speed, the spin bike was relatively quiet, so I played videogames with our kids, watched shows with them sitting on the couch next to me, and conducted "research" on eating and drinking on the bike. Also coincidentally, biking fifty miles happened to take as long as a full length movie!

Though I was now exhausted at the end of movies, I was worried about the swim.

"You should be, you've been riding your old bike to work and running for five months at this point, but when was the last time you ever swam in any sort of competition?"

"Hey, I swam in a sprint triathlon four years ago."

"Yeah, let's see, you never swam in high school or college. The only training beyond what your father had taught you as a kid was in Boy Scouts wasn't it?"

"I can learn."

"You aren't a real swimmer."

"Unlike you, I am real, and I do know how to swim. Therefore, I am a real swimmer."

"You know who you'll be competing with on the swim right? Remember in his book, <u>Finding Ultra</u>, when Rich Roll wrote about all of his swim practices, and about swimming in college at Stanford? Yeah, that's who you'll be swimming against. That's a real swimmer."

"Some people just swim faster than others. If you know how to swim, you are a real swimmer."

"Where do you think you are even going to train?"

"I have a swimming pool."

"Oh yeah, you mean the one your dad warned you would regret buying?"

"Having a swimming pool was one of my life's dreams. When I was eighteen years old I wrote that someday I would own my own swimming pool and I accomplished that dream when you told me I couldn't."

"Oh, you're like Mr. I-Follow-My-Dreams eh?"

"I don't like how you said that. You make it sound like I'm just following some whimsy. I am ignoring you and actively *hunting* my dreams because they reflect who I am trying to become."

"Riiight, like in your kiddy pool?"

"It's not just for my kids to play in; I'm going to train in it."

"Oh, ok. Let's see, it's like thirty feet long, and when you push off the wall you can glide almost halfway across. That's probably the best way to train for swimming in a lake. I'm sure you'll just glide halfway across the lake."

"I won't push off the walls."

"Sure you won't. You're going to train for a 1.2 mile, and then a 2.4 mile swim in a thirty foot pool?"

"Yes."

"Do you even know how many times you'll have to swim across your pool to reach a mile?"

"No. But I'll figure it out."

"Okay, when you do that, be sure to subtract any distance you pushed off a wall."

"Fine. You know what? I'm going to swim circles so I don't get tempted to push off the wall."

"Good idea, I've heard that swimming in a straight line is a really underutilized technique in triathlons. You'll really want to practice swimming in circles instead. Calculate how many circles add up to a mile."

"Fine, I'll just swim by time. If it takes an hour to swim a mile I'll just spend an hour in the pool, and after this race, I'll increase it to two hours or whatever for the next one."

"Well, it sounds like you just have everything figured out. Oh, one other question: how are you going to stay warm? Just because you live in Florida, it is still February, and the water is just fifty degrees."

I really hated these arguments. But there were real obstacles in my way. And they challenged me to decide if I really, really wanted to reach my goals, or if I just thought I did. Unless I tried to do something beyond what I had already mastered I wouldn't grow.

Luckily there was always another force opposing these doubts that seemed to want to help me. It had helped me find that spin bike. Many times it was manifested through my friends. I told a few of them about my worries about the swim.

One of them said, "No problem, I don't like cold water either. Want to use my waterskiing wetsuit?"

Another told me about a local heated swimming pool with fifty yard lanes where I could practice swimming.

When I went to the heated swimming pool, in an embarrassed voice I asked what the difference was between a lap and a length. The lifeguard, an older man, raised a bushy eyebrow and peered at me over his reading glasses.

"A length is down, a lap is down and back," he said.

"How many laps are in a mile?"

"Sixteen," he said, cocking his head. "Why do you want to swim a mile?"

"Um, I'm training for a race," I said, hurrying past him to the locker rooms. I was afraid he'd ask more questions, and I felt too vulnerable to elaborate, afraid one wrong question might tip my barely balancing resolve right over. It reminded me of Will Smith's in the movie, *The Pursuit of Happyness*, when he tells his son, "If you have a dream, you have to protect it."

There was a caveat however: though I never dreamed of becoming an expert swimmer, in reading about expert performance, one of the critical factors to improving performance was getting "high quality feedback."

After a couple of weeks of swimming on my own I realized that to improve I would have to be humble and vulnerable. It was time to hire some swimming faculty. I tentatively approached one of the resident physicians who had swum competitively in college. Balderston had actually competed in triathlons, and swum in the Olympic trials. He also had the rare balance of teachable humility and mental brilliance. I seldom had to correct his work. Nevertheless, it was tricky to reverse roles and have him be the teacher and me be the student. I told him I had worked my way up to swimming an entire mile.

"Great job!" he said.

"It took me forty five-minutes," I said. "Is that fast?"

Balderston has the broad shoulders of a swimmer, and a methodical way of speaking as if cogs and gears turn when he is choosing his words.

"That is pretty fast," he said in his measured voice, pausing as gears turned and mental files were reviewed before gently smiling, "for a person who is a non-swimmer."

"What's fast for a swimmer?" I asked. I had read that the average for the 2.4 mile swim of an Ironman was about eighty minutes, so I thought that forty five was pretty good for a little less than half of that.

"Well, Phelps can do it in about fifteen minutes."

"How fast can you do it?"

"My fastest mile was around sixteen minutes."

I couldn't help but let out a low whistle. Yep, compared to those kinds of times, I was a non-swimmer. I asked if he could give me some tips.

A couple of weeks later, we met at the pool.

Balderston asked me to swim a lap so that he could see what I was doing. Feeling nervous and rather vulnerable to have one of the people I train suddenly training me, I swam as fast as I could. He swam along watching me.

When I got back to him, he smiled. "That was faster than a 45-minute mile."

"Hey, you were watching me. I had to bring my best."

"Ok," he said "Well, there are a few things I noticed that might be helpful."

He pointed out that when I kicked with my legs I bent my knees, probably because of ingraining the movement with all the running I'd been doing. He told me to imagine that my shoulders and torso were making a hole in the water for the rest of my body to fit through.

"If you bend your knees so that they come out of that streamlined hole, then they create drag."

He told me to practice swimming by only flipping my legs from my hips, and minimizing the bend in my knees. Then he reminded me that because I would be using my legs so much during the rest of the race, that I should try to just use my arms as much as possible, so that my legs were rested.

"You want to kick just enough to keep your legs up and inside that hole in the water. You propel yourself with your hands, forearms, and arms. They'll recover during the bike and run portion, so don't worry about them."

Balderston took an hour from his busy schedule to teach me. After the swim session, I sat in my car and wrote down all the things that he had said. It was the most specific and helpful swim instruction I had received in my life. Seeking it had required reserves of humility and vulnerability I didn't know I had in me.

When I saw you, I fell in love, and you smiled because you knew.
William Shakespeare

*Because of you I can feel myself slowly but surely becoming
the me I have always dreamed of being.*
Tyler Knott Gregson, Poet

MILE 17
Break Your Heart until it Opens

Sarang: (Korean) (n) Love.

I had one month until the "Full" Ironman. As I increased my training, I spent even more time alone. My thoughts and mind spun around and around like the wheels on my bike. As I pedaled forward, I thought backward to when I returned from my mission in Brazil. I started dating again at the age of twenty-one. I was searching for someone whose demons would play well with mine. I wasn't expecting someone whose angels would fall in love with my demons.

My father gave me some advice. He said, "As you look for someone to date, look for someone you can run with."

When I met my wife, and we started dating, she asked what I was looking for in a girl.

"I want someone who is intelligent, athletic, and ambitious," I said.

She told me that to make her fall in love I had to make her laugh. But I found that every time she laughed, I was the one who fell further in love. When we were dating, she set up residence in what became both the brightest and the most bewildering place in my heart. I became lost in the smell of her hair, the warm life in her little hands, the feel of her waist turning as we learned to dance, the softness of her mouth, and that feeling in the middle of a kiss when I could feel her smiling.

I remembered what my father taught me, and I believed that the physical prowess that worked so well with other men would work with her. When we were engaged, I asked Katie if we could spend our honeymoon riding our bikes across the United States.

She repeated my request back to me as if she hadn't heard me, or as if I had not heard myself.

"You want to spend our honeymoon biking across the United States?" She crinkled her nose.

"Yes," I replied, grinning.

She looked at me, laughed her beautiful laugh, and shook her mane of dark hair "No."

There is a saying, "A weak man can't love a strong woman. He won't know what to do with her." From experience, I found that as a weak man, I would try to change her.

I spent years of our marriage trying to persuade, beg, guilt-trip, wheedle, pressure, cajole, coax, coerce, and bribe my wife Katie to run with me. There were a few weeks during medical school when she jogged with me, if I would push our kids in a jogging stroller. She looked incredible: her straight back, her smooth stride, her vulnerable determination. As the parade of sick patients increased their pace through my exam rooms, my own desire to exercise increased its pace and affected my relationship with my wife.

In high school when she had vulnerably tried out for track she had been cut. Her heart and resolve broke. When I met her, she did not have a demon pushing her from inside to run, just the opposite. In some ways, I became that demon; she ran for me. Over time this attempt had the opposite effect: instead of leading to closeness between us, it magnified her own insecurities and became too painful.

As I began my semester of experiments my motives were entwined with my relationship with my wife. Some rested on my desire to win her heart and affection. Men do crazy things to try to impress women. After sixteen years of marriage, I was still trying to win her love, to impress her, to prove to her she had bet on a winning horse. Thankfully she is hard to impress, which contributed to me pushing myself harder and harder.

Katie expected more from me because she was willing to give more of herself for me. I wanted to be everything she didn't know she was looking for; to be a man of such a rare quality that if I died, I would be irreplaceable. After the first Around the Bay Relay, when Katie looked at me and said she was proud of me, I cried. I had worked so hard to make her proud of the me she had married, and give her hope for the me I was trying to become. I wanted her to be married to an Ironman.

I believed I couldn't have a good time without thinking how the good time would be great if I was having it with her. When I was running, I thought of her. I imagined her running along beside me. When I was biking, I imagined her riding along with me. In a private part of me I had a fantasy that maybe, through my example, the fire that had caught me would catch her as well. I dreamed of her thinking, "Well, if Travis can run this many miles, I can run at least a few…" In a sense, it was the ultimate experiment, this time, not on myself, but on my wife.

I read somewhere once "when you put two broken people together they either fix each other or break each other further." I am a broken person and in my attempt to "fix" her, I broke myself even further. As the semester wore on and on, I broke over and over, but I always loved Katie with all of my broken pieces. Eventually, I found that only in breaking my body could I fix my broken mind of this crazy idea: she was not going to change. And I did not need her to change in order to change myself.

I believe one of the reasons I was so desperate for her company was I wanted to shift the burden of my loneliness off my own mind. As the miles wore on and on, I began to become more comfortable with my own loneliness, my own skin and my own mind. Mandy Hale once said, "Until you get comfortable with being alone, you'll never know if you're choosing someone out of love or loneliness."

As I continued to push myself, I thought of what the Sufi mystic Rumi had taught, "Your task is not to seek love, but merely to seek and find all the barriers within yourself that you have built against it." Those barriers within my heart were precisely what I was trying to break.

It was difficult to hold myself to my own expectations to exercise, and to eat differently, and not have the intensity of my expectations bleed over into my relationships with other people; with my wife, kids, residents, friends, and patients. Thomas Merton once said, "The beginning of love is to let those we love be perfectly themselves, and not to twist them to fit our own image. Otherwise we love only the reflection of ourselves we find in them." It was strange that I wanted to admire in her what I wanted to admire in myself. What I had imagined I wanted in a girl—intelligence, athleticism, and ambition—were the traits I cultivated in myself!

I struggled to understand that the things I felt called to might not be calling to other people. The Indian guru Osho taught, "If you love a flower, don't pick it up. Because if you pick it up it dies and it ceases to be what you love. So if you love a flower, let it be. Love is not about possession. Love is about appreciation."

Or, as Oscar Wilde put it, "Women are meant to be loved, not to be understood."

I found that my relationship with my wife didn't hurt, my expectations did. When I directed my expectations of myself only toward myself, they could help me become better. When I directed them at others, they could make me bitter.

"Let go or be dragged," says the Zen proverb. I was learning this didn't just apply to material stuff, and the need to travel light, but also to my own mind. I had to let go of my wife. I let her go: on exercise, on diet, on athletic expectation. I cannot change her,

I can only love her. For reasons I didn't understand, her curiosity called her to different paths.

There is a part of my personality that craves validation. I don't know why I am so hungry for it, why I have such holes in my heart for love to leak out of. But it drives me for improvement. It was mystifying that my wife did not want to be the center of attention. She didn't want to be the flower: with its audacious color beaming back at the sun. She wanted to be the invisible root, the source of nourishment and support.

Once I was able to let her go, or rather let go of my expectations, Katie was now freed to share with me her own gifts. When the semester began she agreed to support me, and the time it would take me away from our family, but she would not allow me to use my fatigue, hunger, or pain to justify being a grump. By not allowing grumpiness, self pity, or complaining, she taught me how to be outwardly tougher than I might have been if she had coddled me. Freed to be herself, Katie was able to show me the strength of her gentleness.

As the blood of a marathoner flowed in my veins, there was magic in my wife's heritage as well. In 1998 an ancient tomb was excavated in Korea. In it, archaeologists found a coffin of a man accompanied with a heart-wrenching love letter from his wife dated June 1, 1586. Beside his head, along with the letter, she had placed sandals she had woven from her own hair for his journey. Similarly, once I let go, my wife was free to offer the best of herself to support my journey.

Katie taught me that I don't have to turn everything into a physically punishing challenge. A honeymoon doesn't have to be a bike ride across America. When we were first married she taught me I can use lotion, and Chap Stick. I don't have to sleep in a sleeping bag on the floor, or eat food out of cans or boxes. I don't have to always live a life of Spartan asceticism. Like most women, Katie is sensitive. She over thinks every little thing and cares about the people in her life way too much, and that is precisely what makes her love so strong. She can sense my emotions, and at times is more sensitive to them than I am myself. In this way she reminded me of my own mother pushing back against my father's desire to stay in Alaska. She saw no beauty in willfully and intentionally making life harder and darker and colder than it had to be.

When I was hungry, my natural inclination was to turn it into a fast. I told myself I needed to let my body practice going without glycogen, to burn fat. It would help me lose weight; becoming lighter would help my speed. Katie would ask how much I had eaten and she would be the voice that gave me permission to eat food. If she approved of it, then I didn't feel like I was failing or cheating by taking care of myself.

When my shoes were wearing out my natural inclination was to neither complain nor spend money, but to try to keep going despite the constant annoyance I felt. Katie would laugh and say of course I could buy a new pair of running shoes, or new socks, or new tires for my bike. She encouraged me to buy new songs for my running playlist, and understood when I wanted to buy more puncture resistant tires for my bike to try to prevent another disabling flat tire. When I was exhausted after my long Saturday training sessions but trying to still put on a brave face and be a husband and father, she would tell me to go take a nap.

When I tried to turn my labored loneliness into simple solitude, she would reach out to offer me company instead. When I struggled with my self-doubts, the best compromise I could make with them was to attempt to learn humility. Katie, however, was the voice of affirmation against them. She reminded me to unwind, to be gentle with myself when I was winding myself too tight. Katie allowed me to be hard on myself, but she also protected me from being too hard. After every heartbreaking run, she was there to hug my excavated shell of a body so tight that the pieces of my brokenness stuck back together. As I lost body fat I became colder at night, and she was my warmth. When Katie treated me this way, it was as if God was forgiving me for being the imperfect mess that I am. In the words of Emery Allen: "Having your wounds kissed by someone who doesn't see them as disasters in your soul but cracks to put their love into is the most calming thing in this world."

"When there are two choices, why do you always insist on taking the harder one?" I imagined her asking.

"Why do you assume I see…" I started to say, before she would interrupt.

"You know, being gentle with yourself isn't self-indulgent. Sometimes taking care of yourself is the only way *to* endure."

I thought of the similarities between sports and marriage. For some people, marriage is a sprint and then it is over. For other people, it is an endurance sport, and they are in it for the long haul. I believe that couples who are "meant to be" are the ones who are willing to scale all the brick walls around their dream marriage. They are willing to go through all the obstacles, all the hills, everything that threatens to tear them apart precisely because that is how they learn how strong their love really is.

In my practice of medicine, I saw countless women who out-lived their husbands. On one of the nights when my legs twitched so much that they woke me, I looked over at Katie's beautiful sleeping body. I imagined her out-living me, and sleeping curled up alone. In that moment, I loved her more intensely than any pain I ever felt. I bowed my head and vowed that I would do everything I could to take good care of my health so I would not leave her alone.

Don't you dare shrink yourself for someone else's comfort.
Do not become small for people who refuse to grow.
Marina V, Poet

It's okay to be scared. Being scared means you're about to do
something really, really brave.
Mandy Hale, Author

MILE 18
Swimming with Alligators

Palinoia: (Greek) (n). The obsessive repetition of an act until it is perfected or mastered.

Running step after step for hours is mind-numbing stuff. I dealt with it by focusing on the terrain, or the dogs, or the music. Biking along in my living room with my family had plenty of mental distraction. Swimming, with the floating sensation, the horrible featurelessness of the black line on the bottom of the lane staring up at me and the water silencing everything amplified the loudness of the voice in my own mind. This made it incredibly difficult to keep count of laps and lengths. I began swimming holding up a certain number of fingers. Balderston dropped a triathlon wetsuit off at my office. Unlike the waterskiing one, its seams were perfectly smooth. He had cut off the lower parts of the legs, explaining that they had made the suit really difficult to get out of quickly at the transition areas.

"This will give your legs some buoyancy, so they'll be easier to keep in line with your body," he said.

I could run or ride for hours because I had things to distract me, but swimming was mentally brutal. As I swam circles in my own freezing swimming pool wearing both wetsuits, the mindlessness left claw marks from my mind trying to escape itself. I knew for some people, the mindlessness of repetition was a barrier for running. This is also a barrier that keeps some people from meditation, or from prayer. Somehow I had overcome this barrier with some activities, but with swimming I had not.

I drew strength from a story about this particular kind of hell. Sisyphus was a character in one of the ancient Greek tragedies who was punished by the gods. Each day he had to roll a large boulder up a hill, only to watch it roll back down and then have to do it all over again the next day. Besides swimming back and forth for hours, or around and around for hours, there were other things in my own life that felt like boulders. Every time I got through all the new lab results for my patients, they filled right back up. Every time I finished seeing a clinic full of patients and thought I was done and had fixed them, new patients were waiting for me the next day. No matter how hard I pushed, the boulders were always waiting for me the next day.

On one level, the myth of Sisyphus is one of undying hopelessness, of eternal nihilism. But, looked at another way, it is a story of incredible hope. Each time Sisyphus pushed and heaved that boulder to the top of the hill he was triumphant.

"Rock, you don't own me!" I imagine him shouting from the top of the hill watching the boulder roll back down, "I just owned you! AGAIN!!"

I imagine his confident booming laugh chasing the boulder back down the hill.

Another length, another lap. Another mile. I tried to laugh a booming laugh, but I was too busy trying to ensure my breathing was organized with my strokes.

"Make sure you practice breathing from both sides," my father told me on our weekly phone call, "you won't have a black line to follow during the race, so you have to be able to find the buoy when your head comes up to breathe."

A couple of days before the race, my wife took my bike to a bike shop to get it tuned-up. The bike guy asked what event I was training for, and she told him. He told her my training was all wrong.

When I got home, one of the tires from his tune up was flat. Despite riding over a thousand miles, I had not had a single flat tire during the entire time I had been training. I hadn't changed a flat in years. Rather than take it back, I changed it myself. One more boulder. One more chance for me to prove how bad I wanted this.

When I registered for this event, the flyer claimed the swim would take place in "certified pristine waters," of central Florida. I imagined crystal blue waters where you could see thirty feet down to the fish swimming over the white sandy bottom of the lake. I imagined a photographer taking pictures of us from below and the water and sky blending together so that we would appear to be swimming across the blue watery sky with the sun.

When we arrived at the course, the "pristine waters" were a dense, murky brown. Signs warned not to feed the alligators.

"With what?" I wondered, "My own body?"

The next morning, I slipped into the wetsuit, and pulled the long string on the back to zip it up. Fit looking people milled around in their wetsuits getting their race numbers inked on their muscled arms and greeting each other with expressions of familiarity. Expensive, featherweight bikes waited impatiently in the transition areas. My own bike leaned against the rack in a tired, but sturdy sort of way. I set my shorts, running shoes, and socks next to it along with a bucket of water to rinse my feet, and walked down to the lake. I looked out at the lake as the sun rose. The bright inflatable buoy that marked the halfway turn-around point floated impossibly far out in the distance. Two canoes and a fishing boat lined the course. I wondered if they scared off the alligators or attracted them. I hoped the fishing boat wasn't chumming.

When the gun finally went off, people sprinted into the water and started swimming over and through each other. I waded in at a gentle jog, letting the speediest people go first. It would be hard enough to see in that dark water, I didn't want my goggles to get kicked off too. I took one last look at the buoy floating on the horizon to orient myself and dived in. My parents taught me to swim when I was just a little kid, and I've never had fears of swimming, but when I entered the water, stared down into the blackness and was unable to see my arm pass beneath me, I felt curiously afraid.

The wet, bubbly sounds of swimming sloshed rhythmically around me. Steadily that watery cadence coalesced into familiar sounds.

"Will you even be able to see an alligator in this?"

Time your breathing with your strokes.

"How deep do you think they swim?"

Alternate breathing on either side. Breathe on the left this time.

"An alligator's eyes are on top of its head, so it is probably swimming below you looking up at you. How big do they get?"

Pull with your hands and forearms.

"Do you think they use the sun above you to silhouette you through all this darkness?"

Keep your head down and legs up, like you are swimming downhill. Kick from the hips.

"Everyone else is way ahead of you. Alligators probably don't like that big group. Think they'll pick off the slow stragglers in the back?"

Something grabbed my hand.

"What the heck was that?" I almost shot out of the water.

The wetsuit's long zipper string had wrapped around my hand. I flicked it away and kept swimming. It grabbed at me again with the next stroke.

Rotate along the long axis of your body, don't bend side to side or front to back.

"Are you even swimming straight? I bet you aren't even swimming toward the buoy. I bet you're swimming off to one side where you will be alone."

That person swimming ahead is leaving a trail of bubbles. Follow the bubbles.

"Does that person know where they are going?"

Okay, do a few strokes of breaststroke so you can see ahead of you, find the buoy, and catch your breath.

"You're almost in the middle of this lake. How deep do you think this water is? If you drown, do you think they'd even be able to find your body?"

For a brief moment, staring down into the wet, unmoving darkness below me, my thoughts, like vicious alligators overwhelmed me. I felt panic. I flipped over to my back and stared up at the bright sky with its rising sun. I swam the backstroke, caught my breath and let the panic wash away. It probably took five strokes to steady myself. Then, I flipped back over and continued swimming to the buoy. When I finally saw the buoy's lofty inflated redness loom into view, my mind steadied briefly.

I swam back to the shore chased by my crazy thoughts.

"Remember the newspaper article that said people had been releasing their pet Burmese pythons into the everglades and how they have totally taken over? Do snakes swim?"

The zipper string tried to hold my hand again. I flicked it away. It was insistent. I flicked it away.

"Is that guy gaining on you?"

The faster you swim, the faster you get away from the alligators.

"Don't some of these lakes have that amoeba that gets in your nose and eats your brain?"

Remember to use this swim for practice for the next race; it's going to be twice as long. This is just practice.

I got to the end of the swim, and staggered up on the sandy beach. I passed the timer, finishing the swim in thirty-nine minutes. People told me to lie down on a mat and they'd help me get the wetsuit off. They unzipped it and peeled it from my shoulders all the way down. I desperately grabbed for my underwear to keep them from going off too.

Carrying the wetsuit like a deflated friend, I ran gingerly on bare feet to the transition area, which I noticed was missing most of the bikes. I threw on my shorts and shirt, stepped into my bucket, rinsed my feet, and put on my socks and shoes. I trotted the bike to the end of the transition area, fastened my helmet, and took off. After seeing me off, my wife went back to the hotel to eat and get our kids so they could watch the end of the bike and then the final run portion.

The ride started out nice, and cyclists stretched ahead of me for miles. After a few minutes I found my rhythm and almost relaxed into enjoying it. The course wound along back roads, past beautiful houses and fields. The road twisted around corners and rolled up hills. There were a few bike water bottles littering the way. I tried to eat, to get some calories in me while my stomach wasn't bouncing, so that I would be ready for the run. I passed a rider who had wrecked some minutes before. His front rim was bent. Blood dripped from his shredded biking shorts down to his knee. He sat at the side of the road waving us on and talking on a cell phone. I felt really sad for him, he had probably been training for months and now it was over.

The halfway point was right after the steepest hill climb of the ride which left my legs burning. The fire in my thighs was so painful I wasn't sure I'd be able to pedal, or if I'd be forced to hike the rest of the hill pushing my bike like Sisyphus's boulder.

As I neared the top my front tire began feeling mushy. I looked down at it, and watched the rubber flatten against the road. I cursed the bike shop owner and everyone who ever said it was a good idea to have your bike tuned up before a race. I wished I'd had a phone with me so I could call Katie, but I had left it behind. I didn't want to be disqualified for having a device that could also play music. The tire went completely flat right as I pulled into a race aid station where cyclists were handed bananas and drinks of water or sports drinks. I asked the volunteers if any of them had a pump. Bikes whizzed by. Nobody had a pump.

A group of cyclists who were not part of the race pulled up to a stop at the next house. I asked if any of them had a pump. One of them said she had some CO_2 canisters. The strange blessing of having a flat from the tune-up was that I was able to change the tire quickly.

As I pulled away, thanking them for their help, I cursed myself for not being prepared. Over the years I had frequently allowed myself to feel disappointed in my medical patients who didn't put in the effort to learn how their own bodies worked, or how to take care of themselves, and yet, I had shown the same abdication of responsibility when it came to taking care of my own bike. We have a responsibility to master our own stuff.

My father-in-law is building his own airplane in his garage. When I asked him about why he was doing it, he answered, "Hey,

I could hire someone to do this, but when I'm flying I want to know every single rivet is in correctly."

My bike has thirty-two spokes on each tire. I had sent it to be tuned up because I didn't want to tighten all of them. When the bike guy had tightened them he had left off the piece of tape that lines the inside of the tire rim and covers the holes where the spokes enter. Not counting these spokes, my bike only has thirty screws. I should have been able to tune all of them myself. We need to know our own bodies, and we need to know our own bikes. After the miles and hours we spent together, I had neglected one area of necessary knowledge for this semester. I had faith in my trusty old steed, but I had not taken complete ownership.

When I finally dropped my bike off at the final transition area, I was nowhere near the front. People had been faster than me on the swim, and though I had passed many people on the bike, my flat tire had set me back considerably.

When I got to the run portion of the triathlon, I was surprised to see how many people were walking. Their legs were just fried from the bike ride. I had learned that most marathoners walk at least part of their races, and certainly most people walked portions of ultras, but this was only a half marathon! Running and biking use different muscles, but at the same time, endurance is endurance. I had to admit, my own legs were tired, but because I had been running to work, and then running home, I was used to running on tired legs. So while the competitors around me mixed running with walking, I ran. Thirteen miles is not fifty. I don't know how many people I passed, but no one passed me on the run.

Behind every young man who believes in himself
is a parent who believed in him first.
Matthew Jacobsen

Small boys become big men through the influence of
big men who care about small boys.
Anonymous

MILE 19
Declaration of Imperfection

Incalescent: (Latin) (adj) growing hotter or more ardent; set ablaze.

Around mile twenty is where most runners "hit the wall." When this happened to me, my thoughts turned dark and broody, and minor nuisances were amplified into full irritants. Libba Bray taught that our minds are not cages, they are gardens, which require cultivating. Sometimes there are shadowy areas in those gardens, and fatigue made these shadows stretch. In these times I found myself being upset with my patients for being sick and hurt, and this extended to being upset with them for being imperfect. I was upset with their parents. Why didn't their parents teach them how to take better care of themselves? Sometimes I would become upset with myself, and my own parents, and their parents. I ran in the shadow of these unhelpful thoughts and wondered why it was dark. What were the origins of my voices of angry expectation? When I turned them on myself why did they lead to my own self-doubts and addiction?

In my times of fatigue, I ran and I thought about my parents' flaws. I thought of my wife's faults. I thought about my imperfect siblings. I thought with impatience about patients who refused vaccines, and about the mistakes the residents made as they learned to practice medicine. I thought about the mistakes I had made, and about the times when the other faculty (or even worse—residents!) found mistakes I had made. I swam and I thought about how flawed my swimming form probably was.

Every few years I work up the courage ask God if I could know Him. In response, I am reminded of my own imperfections. Perhaps these are what keep me from knowing Him, or perhaps these are the answer I didn't know I was actually looking for. Perhaps imperfections are the places He is most needed, the places where He lives.

My angry thoughts about people left me hollowed out, like an empty wetsuit. In the end, the only path I could find that led to peace of mind was forgiveness. I had to forgive so much imperfection. I read somewhere once that "withholding forgiveness is like serving a prison sentence for a crime you didn't commit. It is like drinking poison and hoping the other person will die."

So many times as I ran, I was haunted by the fact that my run times might not be as fast as those of other people; my distances might not be as far. The voices of self-doubt were always with me, but as I studied them, I realized that much of their chanting was directed at comparing me to perfection. And in the words of Brene' Brown, "when perfectionism is driving... shame is always riding shotgun."

"If you can't win these events, or do something for the first time, you shouldn't even do it," said my voices of doubt.

I stole a reply from Elizabeth Gilbert, "I never said I would do it perfectly, I only said I was going to do it."

And so, one day, as I ran, I made a Declaration of Imperfection. I made it to give myself psychological breathing room. I had to forgive my residents, my crazy family, my wife, my parents, my patients, my kids and myself. I had to give room to be imperfect. After getting cancer, Regina Brett wrote that we must forgive everyone everything. And we don't forgive people because they did anything to deserve it, but forgive because we deserve to have peace.

As I exercised and pursued this elusive thing called "fitness" I changed my prayer and prayed to see my patients as God does. I wanted to see them with His eyes. I wanted to see past their diseases and resistance to change and see them with wonder and love. As part of my Declaration of Imperfection, I also had to make this declaration on behalf of my patients. To let go of hurt I had to learn to love and admire them despite their imperfections, and see them as good people who were worth loving. I learned to forgive their imperfect parents. It dawned on me that imperfections are simply one more brick wall, one more obstacle to be overcome. But expecting perfection was also a huge obstacle. I had to accept that making mistakes was better than faking perfection. Sometimes what I considered a mistake was simply the unexpected result of some experiments anyway.

As I shielded them behind this declaration, I came to see my patients who smoked not as people who were trying to get cancer to make more sadness and work for me, but rather as people who were hurting and stressed out and turned to something to calm themselves down. I came to see patients who struggled with their weight as people who were hurting and who turned to food to lift their spirits. I came to see that addicts are my people. Their standing as legitimate and beloved members of my tribe was just as valid as the standing of my athletic friends.

When I accepted my own imperfections and worked to forgive myself, it was liberating. I don't have to be a perfect runner to run. I don't have to be a perfect writer to write. I don't have to be a perfect man to be a husband and father. I don't have to be a perfect physician to be a surgeon. I don't have to be tramping through a perfect jungle in a perfect khaki shirt to be an explorer. Explorers are allowed to make mistakes. In fact, the very calling is predicated on having an imperfect understanding and on not knowing something so that it must be explored. Exploring isn't about perfection; it is about watching and learning, and feeling awe. I could explore endurance and pain and loneliness. I could explore my relationship with my father, and my father's father.

As the bright edges of this declaration expanded and chased away the shadows of my mind, it covered my father as well. Like anybody, I don't always understand my dad. I could never know the doubts that whirled about him and rode him and drove him. Many of them came from the emotional earthquake in his family that occurred when he was only sixteen and his father had a heart attack. I imagined him as a teen-ager being told that death's sickle hung over his beloved father at all times now. I imagine a sixteen year old young man bracing himself to shoulder responsibility for his mother and two sisters when that sickle fell. I imagine the fear whispering to him that his father would die. I imagine my father kneeling down at night and praying for his father's broken heart, and praying for strength for himself.

I imagine him as a young father, and the fear of failing my mom and eight dependent kids. He was busy at work, and his attention was divided eight different ways when he was home. I imagine his need to get away and clear his head and run. Maybe, like me, having physical victories was his one way to have any victories some days. When he ran marathons, the point of doing something great was not to make others feel bad or to brag. It is to quiet our own demons and to inspire others.

When he asked me to be better than he had been, perhaps it was because he was having one of those days when he was feeling the lonely weight of his own imperfections. Maybe my father's runs were his answers to the voices and demons he wrestled with. Maybe, when I invited him to share the semester and he reminded me of my familial responsibilities he wasn't even speaking to me, maybe he was just speaking to his own demons that told him he hadn't been a good enough father. Maybe the only thing that had kept him from devoting all the hours necessary to do an Ironman when he was younger had been his devotion to supporting his family. Maybe what he had told me that day was simply a repetition of a mantra he had told himself over the years to keep his own balance. As I came to understand these things, when I made a Declaration of Imperfection for my father, I came to realize that in his own imperfect way, he did his absolute best, which in its own way was a form of perfection!

Throughout my life, every time we visited my grandfather, my dad warned us that this visit might be the last time we saw him. I learned that I also had to forgive my grandfather for having a heart attack and how this affected my father his whole life. To do this, I couldn't just declare that "Oh well, he was imperfect." I had to understand the context, origins, and explanations of his flaws.

My grandfather grew up during the Great Depression. He was one of twelve kids, though only seven made it to adulthood. I cannot imagine conditions where almost half your family dies. When he left home, he took one critical lesson with him: work hard and work smart. He went to work shoveling coal on an oil-freighter. I imagine him covered in black coal dust deep in the bowels of the freighter creaking across the pacific. When he learned that the ship's engineers had their own cabins, a novelty he had never had in his life, my grandfather bought the engineering textbooks when he was in port. When they set out to sea again, he set out to memorize all the engineering equations. With black fingers on a blackboard, I imagine him writing another equation with a piece of white chalk to memorize by the light of the boilers. He shoveled fire across the oceans, and he fed the fire of his mind as well. For my grandfather, endurance events weren't for sport or fitness; they were they physical toll he paid to make a better life for himself and his future family, including me.

After years at sea, and after shoveling literally tons of coal, he took the engineering licensing exam and passed without ever going to college. He used that to go to work for US Steel, and then went on to work for NASA during the mercury missions. It was just like using one race to prepare for the next one. It was when he worked for NASA that he had his first heart attack. Looking at how physically demanding his life had been up to that point, and the types of rations he must have lived on, it is no surprise that he had a heart attack. It was the price he willingly paid to leave his legacy.

My father once wrote about it, "When I was a high school sophomore, and he was forty-nine, my dad had his first heart attack. He was out of work for eight weeks to recover. I will never forget how my dad coped with this life-threatening event during those weeks: he started to exercise. For him exercise meant running. Looking back, I remember teasing him that he looked kind of funny when he ran. Perhaps because of being teased, he was always self-conscious about running where anyone might see him. So, he ran inside the house. Dad would run down the hall from his bedroom through the dining room and then down the hall by the three of us kids' bedrooms, then through the living room and then back down the other hall by his and Mom's room. He calculated that he had to run this loop sixty-three times to equal one mile. The unique thing about my dad's running was he always did it in his underwear. So as I was getting up for early morning seminary I had to be on the lookout for dad running over me as he jogged around the halls in his drawers. As crazy as it sounds, and though my dad wore the carpets out and we had to replace them, my father actually lost twenty pounds by running miles inside the house. My father's heart attack shook all of us, and so as a high school student, I had my cholesterol checked as well. The doctor told me that my cholesterol was borderline high and that I should try to make sure I was always employed somewhere where I could be physically active. I started running track and cross-country around this time, though unlike my father, I wore proper running clothes. Though he had lost weight, additional heart attacks became a common theme for the rest of my father's life. They happened so often that we thought he might die at any time, but medicine kept advancing. Surgeons developed the coronary artery bypass graft, and a vein from his leg was attached to bypass the blockages in four vessels of his heart, and amazingly he kept going until he was eighty-seven."

I had to forgive my grandfather for having a heart attack and scaring—and scarring—my father. He worked hard his whole life to lift himself and his family into a better life. I had to forgive my dad for his charge when I was just a boy. He doesn't even remember it anymore. Sometimes parents tell kids stories, and sometimes kids tell themselves stories. As I've reflected back on it, I've wondered if that day even happened, or if it was simply a story I told myself when I was four…

I hadn't considered how much my own actions might have hurt my father. I had to consider how much I needed him to forgive me. I realized I don't want to compete with my father's legacy anymore. When we compete with others we risk becoming either proud or bitter. When we compete with ourselves, we become either humbler or better. I want them to run their own runs.

I thought of my vision of the ghosts of all my dead ancestors running with me. Death is a kind of finish line. There is part of me that is so tired and wants to reach it to rest. And there is part of me that realizes I need to keep running through that finish line also, because one day my ghost will run with my children and their children. I had to consider that one day my father's ghost would run with me as well.

As I continued training and running, I imagined my grandfather's ghost running along with me, telling me to keep going, that I was capable of pushing harder than that. His ghost would be shouting that he had left me the wells of greater strength than I had tapped into yet, that I was not the heir of softness, but of coal-fired strength.

Though I had never seen it in my lifetime, I knew that I would recognize his ghost by his unusual gait.

And that he ran in his underwear.

If you raise your children to feel that they can accomplish any
goal or task they decide upon,
you will have succeeded as a parent and you will have given your
children the greatest of all blessings.
Brian Tracy, Author

You are the poem I never knew how to write
and this life is the story I have always wanted to tell.
Tyler Knott Gregson, Poet

MILE 20
Redemption, Not Insurrection

Napenthe: (Greek) (n) something that can make you forget grief or suffering.

At the time of my semester, my son was fifteen, and my daughter was twelve. In the words of Robert Fulghum, I didn't worry that my children weren't listening to me. I was worried that they were always watching me. And I was worried that they spelled love T-I-M-E. As I spent more and more time training, it became like having a part time job on top of an already busy profession. I worried about what sort of a father I was being. Over the miles and miles my father's warning echoed hauntingly after me down the sidewalks and streets. His example left a silhouette in my eyes the way staring at a bright light burns ghosts in the vision. His words joined the choir of my own voices of doubt and emerged sounding like this:

"Do you think your children will tell the same story about this that you are telling yourself?"

In many ways, on the days they were born, I began turning into a ghost. In the words of Jerry Seinfield, "Make no mistake about why these babies are here—they are here to replace us." They were the present and the future. Their births sentenced me to the past. From this curious position I still wanted to communicate with these miraculous beings that would run past me into the future. I wanted them to take the best of me with them.

I had passed the story and the charge on to my son and daughter. I had told them that I expected them to be better than me. I told my son when he was only four years old. I remember how the small bones of his shoulders stirred underneath my hands. He looked up at me with the tearful determination of a child whose dad was asking too much of him and he told me he would try. In giving him the charge, I had bound myself to helping him. I closed my eyes for a moment and suddenly, where my little son had been, a young man stood before me. His shoulders were now firm, confident, and he smiled.

One minute my tiny daughter is laying in my armpit, pointing a chubby finger at the words of Dr. Seuss, sounding out the letters, because I vowed that she will be better prepared for school than I had been. The next minute I was waking up and she was reading the last book on her shelves, turning the pages faster than I could keep up.

"Squashy," I whispered to her, studying the incredible way that her face mixed her mother's face with remnants of my own.

"Yes dad."

"When you grow up, you need to be intelligent, athletic and ambitious, ok?"

"I'm like you dad, but I'm also curious about other stuff."

Without my awareness, my son signed up for cross country in the sixth grade. My daughter signed up for track, running the four hundred and the anchor for the relay. For years they had watched me return home after running. They recognized, just as I had by watching my father, that running was part of who we were.

"When you are my age, I expect you to be able to do this. This is the standard."

"You sound like Opa."

"Yeah, sometimes when I open my mouth my dad pops out." It made me wonder how many words, how many dreams, and even how many of what I thought were my own thoughts were simply echoes from previous generations. "Did I ever tell you about the time I ran a marathon with Opa?"

"Yeah, we see you wearing the t-shirt dad."

"Well, you know when you are doing the relay and you hand off the baton to the next person and they are usually even faster than you?"

"Yeah."

"Well when I run with Opa, and when you guys ran those parts with me around the bay, it's kind of like that."

"Dad, I'm the last person on the relay because I *am* the fastest."

When my daughter started band and was asked what instrument she wanted to learn to play, she looked at them all, thought for a moment and then asked, "Which one is the hardest?"

I wanted to cry with pride.

I love the French horn, not because of its sound, but because of its difficulty.

When I was four years old my father told me a story. With the shine of sadness in his eyes he told me he expected me to be a better man than he had been. One of our parental responsibilities is to do everything we can to help our children become good people, to fix the weaknesses we might otherwise pass on to them.

I even applied this obligation to the residents I teach. I told them that I expect them to be better physicians than I have been.

"After all," I tell them, "you have a better teacher than I did."

In <u>Battle Hymn of the Tiger Mother</u>, Amy Chua wrote, "American mothers are afraid their children are weak; Chinese mothers know that their children are strong."

As my kids have grown, they have started meeting my pitiless expectation. They began doing many things better than me to our mutual embarrassment. They found my old report cards, and were shocked at my grades. Neither of them had any grade except an A. They teased me about all those *other* letters. I tried to laugh it off, but underneath the words I could hear their surprise: they were actually keeping the charge to be better than me. Who knew it would be so easy?

I did.

I knew it would be because, though I never told them, I would do all that I could to help them achieve the heavy responsibility I had placed on them.

I couldn't go back to fix certain things I had broken in my life, but in my quest to fix my mistakes and weaknesses I could pass on the things I had learned to help make weak areas strong in my children, and in my residents. They didn't know that I had quit running entirely at one point, nor that part of me was doing this semester to try to fix my own weaknesses. As a dad I need my children to be better than I have been, because in helping them to become better, they make me better, too.

My father's charge of expecting me to be better than him was not a charge to lead an insurrection; it was a plea for redemption. I need my kids to be better than me as a way of forgiving myself. Their excellence became both a source of tremendous pride, and also shame that I had not been better. I was not expecting how much it would actually hurt to have my children outgrow me.

I had one last, brutal month until the full monster triathlon. I spoke with my dad about my preparations, and he asked if he could run the second half of the marathon with me. I knew I would be exhausted at that point, and the idea gave my enthusiasm a little boost.

I spent more hours riding the spin bike indoors, which gave me more time to spend with them while I was training. I was home, in the middle of things if someone needed me or wanted me. I watched movies with them. I played video games. My wife took a picture of me riding the bike and playing Halo with my daughter and posted it on Facebook teasing that this was how I was training for an Ironman.

Of course it was! That photo did make me sad, because with a simple stationary bike, video gamers could become synonymous with fitness freaks instead of laziness.

I continued to come home from work, either biking or running most days of the week. After a hard workout some athletes recommend taking ice baths to decrease inflammation. I put on the two wet suits my friends had lent me, and stepped into the fifty degree water of my swimming pool. The legs would initially billow outward, filled with air. Thankfully the extra buoyancy helped hold more of me above icy wetness for a few extra moments as I treaded the water to warm up. Slowly the air hissed upward, followed by a cold, wet chill spreading up my body. Then I would start my circles. I turned the pool filter on high and swam against the current.

Sometimes, my wife would come outside and talk with me as I swam. The dogs watched me from beyond splashing distance. Once or twice the kids would come out and watch or ask me a question. Sometimes I would turn the pool lights out and just swim endless circles in the darkness spiraling into my own mind. Two hours later, when I heaved my dripping, shivering exhaustion from the pool the water drained back out from the legs of the wetsuits, lightening its weight with each sodden step.

To my list of experiments conducted I added this finding: Ice baths do, in fact, work to keep the ache in tired legs numb. Incidentally, they also make the feet numb.

After a warm shower, I would join my family for dinner where I ate until it hurt. I was with my family. I was trying to find the right balance. Alain de Botton once said, "There is no such thing as work-life balance. Everything worth fighting for unbalances your life."

When we try to find a work/family balance, some believe we should always choose the side of spending more time with our families. I have known people who turned down difficult assignments at work that they needed to take to get promoted in the name of "spending time with my family." I have known people who refused to get real, difficult and back-breaking jobs that required mature adult fortitude, by hiding instead behind the guise of "wanting to be there for my children." I do not believe that is the only path, nor that it is always the right path. In the words of Mike Rowe, "I believe that the best way to distinguish myself at work is to show up early, stay late, and cheerfully volunteer for every crappy task there is." Modeling how to do difficult things is part of taking care of our children. When I was growing up I watched my father work long hours. Many times he wasn't around. I suspect that he may have felt guilty about how much time he was absent. He probably worried about how he was doing as a father when he was gone so much. I did not resent his hard work, or his absences. I respected and admired him for it.

When my friend Todd Wendel hiked the Appalachian Trail which runs from Georgia to Maine, he left his wife and sons for over six months to hike. When I asked his wife if she felt bad that he had been gone from them for so long, she said, "Not at all. Sure we missed him, but every day we charted his progress as a family. My sons saw what it really takes to go follow your dreams and to have an adventure. They saw how hard it really was. He left them a legacy and an example of how to do hard things."

I didn't want to simply tell my children to follow their dreams, I wanted to show my children an example of how to methodically and ruthlessly hunt down and conquer a big hairy audacious goal. In their dark and lonely moments, I want them to know deep inside their bones that they are heirs of a legacy from which they can draw strength. I thought of how my reservations about not having any family members who were surgeons had undercut my confidence that I could be a surgeon, or that no one in my family was a writer. I did not want to pass that on.

Because he had left me this legacy, inviting my father to do an Ironman with me seemed like a perfectly reasonable father-son activity. My father had warned me I had other responsibilities. I believe one of our parental responsibilities is to cultivate within our children a knowledge that they are capable of so much more than the world tells them is possible even if that means demonstrating it personally. One of our responsibilities is to expect greatness from them, and then to set such an example that it shows them it is possible. One of our parental responsibilities *is* to follow our dreams.

The unfed mind devours itself.
Gore Vidal, Thinker

Set your life on fire.
Seek those who fan the flames.
Rumi, Sufi mystic

MILE 21
Don't Quit Your Daydream

Lichtenberg figures: (German) (noun) Reddish, fernlike patterns and scars that form on skin struck by lightning.

I didn't understand how sports psychology worked, but as I trained, I began noting my own thought habits. Unfortunately, worries and excuses frequently filled my thoughts. As I continued training for the final event of my semester of experiments, my snickering doubts kept me company. Worries and fears would swell up, gathering mass and audacity until they crashed into me and threatened to sweep me off my course.

"Don't you think the people passing you in their cars are laughing at your gait?"

"Don't you think the people in that car didn't notice you were walking and only started running when you saw them?"

"Don't you think that the car that just passed you could tell your shorts have a hole in them?"

"Did you notice that kid laughing at how you are stopping to pick up your dogs' poop?"

It was exhausting listening to the grate of these thoughts on my mind. I had to carefully and deliberately dilute, destabilize and damage their arguments.

I began waving hello when cars approached. People waved back.

"See, I told you they were watching you."

"They are waving their support of me."

"They were just waving because you did. If they meant it, they would have smiled at you."

I began smiling and waving.

People smiled and waved back.

"You know they are only doing that because you did."

"You don't always tell the truth. You also told me that I would come home exhausted from riding my bike to work, but I experimented and that's not true. I come home in a better mood when I ride my bike than I do when I drive home."

"You know you aren't going to beat anyone at this. These are real competitors, monsters. You are going to get crushed."

"I am not in a competition with anyone. I have no desire to play the game of being better than anyone."

"Then why are you running? Who are you racing with? Who are you trying to beat?"

"I am simply trying to be better than the me I was yesterday."

"Yeah, we remember him; he's that guy who was never the fastest guy on the cross-country team right? We know you."

"No, you knew me, but you don't know me. I am still becoming the me I really am, the me I am supposed to be."

"Wow, that sounds lofty, I bet your kids love having a dad who isn't around and who is always out training."

There is no point in arguing. I turn up my music and run faster. Sometimes I just have to get out of my own way, out of my own head. So, sometimes I use music to blockade my mind against doubts and fatigue. Over the course of the semester I had had to update my running playlist several times just to keep things fresh because the voices of doubt press their whispering lips to any cracks in my resolve. Sometimes the voices of doubt still broke through, and threatened to break my resolve. I had to really focus on why I was doing this. Every runner has a reason.

People frequently said to me, "I could never run a marathon," or, "I could never run an ultramarathon," or "I could never do an Ironman."

To which I replied, "That's because you don't have a *reason* to. If you had a reason to, then of course you could." Frequently people simply did not have enthusiasm to do hard things.

The word "enthusiasm" is from the Greek meaning "filled with God," with the same root as "theos" which gives us "theology" etcetera. In ancient Greece, an "enthusiast" was a person possessed by something divine. To me, my enthusiasm to run was like a little pet that I had to learn how to feed and take care of. When I was tired, discouraged or just did not feel like exercising anymore, I found that I could just recognize and name what I was feeling and it didn't threaten my enthusiasm.

I had learned to feed it books on running. The thoughts, teachings, and triumphs of these writing runners fed, watered, and played with my enthusiasm. I cultivated what I admired, and what I wanted to grow inside of me. When my friends, co-workers and family learned I was going to run fifty miles, they worried I was now possessed, not by a god, but by some variation of madness... some sort of a demon.

Roald Dahl said, "I began to realize how important it was to be an enthusiast in life. If you are interested in something, no matter what it is, go at it full speed ahead. Embrace it with both arms, hug it, love it and above all become passionate about it. Lukewarm is no good. Hot is no good, either. White hot and passionate is the only thing to be."

White hot is the best temperature to cultivate a demon. As I fed books into the furnace to keep my enthusiasm hot I noticed something curious. In Marshall Ulrich's book, *Running on Empty*, he described arriving at the 135 mile Badwater Ultramarathon, the legendary run through Death Valley in August: "I found friends there, people driven by their own demons and dreams, men and women of extraordinary grit and drive and determination." I noticed that many of the people I read about had different demons that drove them. Marshall Ulrich's first wife slowly died of cancer, and he ran further and further until he ran all the way across America, averaging about sixty miles a day. In *Finding Ultra*, Rich Roll wrote about how exercise helped him overcome his alcoholism. Watching his mother become crippled by multiple sclerosis as he grew up haunted ultrarunning legend Scott Jurek in his book *Eat and Run*. David Goggins was haunted by his fellow Navy SEALs who were killed in combat. The shadow of my grandfather's poor health and threat of imminent death haunted my father and became his demon, and fueled his fitness enthusiasm.

I wondered what my own demon was. What were my real reasons for doing this crazy semester of experiments? I ran and rode and swam and thought and trained for the the Ironman distance triathlon. Certainly there was the presence of death and disease. Every patient I have had who has died has scared and driven me to live just a little better. Every patient who comes in and is making poor health choices has frustrated and exhausted me. I love them, and want them to be healthy. I am afraid for them, for their inevitable hypertension-induced strokes and diabetes-induced neuropathy. The fear snaps at me, and I shove back. I want to lead them out of bondage. I want to lead by example so they will at least try. Practicing medicine was my *memento mori*, the Latin phrase, "remember that you will die." I wanted to make myself the hardest target cancer, diabetes, or heart disease ever tried to kill. I wanted my wife and kids and friends to make themselves hard targets as well.

I thought about my kids and about the resident physicians and how much I loved and admired them. I wanted all of them to be better than me. I wanted to put my hands on their shoulders and tell them this crazy expectation. I didn't want my kids to be so afraid, and I didn't want the residents to be eaten by the madness that had overthrown me when I was a resident. And I realized that if I felt that way, then I owed it to them to help. I owed it to them to work harder to leave a worthy example.

Throughout my career I saw people leaving family medicine for "easier" specialties: dermatology, radiology, flight medicine, and even administrative jobs. How could I show them medicine was a great and worthy calling?

After my four years of teaching at the residency program, I was being courted to take a job at another hospital where I would be in charge of both primary care physicians and surgeons. How would the surgeons ever respect me as a leader? I worried that because their residency training was two years longer than mine I would have no phronesis, no "street cred," with them.

I thought about the residents; how they did the majority of the work, and how I sat back and read and double-checked their work, but they did the heavy lifting. My own conscience felt convicted. Having a subordinate work harder than me violated the principles my father had taught me. Leaders were supposed to lead by example.

I thought about how in high school I had only been an average runner, no one special. I thought about my life regrets: I never earned my Eagle Scout despite having my father as my scoutmaster, I never learned German despite living there for nine and half years, I didn't go in to surgery because my fascination was overthrown by my doubts and fears. Each of these regrets was like a nail in the coffin of my dreams of the life I wished I had made for myself.

I thought of what I would do after this semester. What other lives did I want to live?

So, beside books, and magazines, and music and YouTube videos on fitness like "I Am a Champion," I started collecting quotes that inspired me. I wanted to feed the fire of enthusiasm until it was so bright my doubts had no shadows left to hide in.

"A bird sitting on a tree branch is not afraid of the branch breaking. His trust is not in the branch, but in his own wings."

"It had long since come to my attention that people of accomplishment rarely sat back and let things happen to them. They went out and happened to things." Leonardo da Vinci

"I want to live and feel all the shades, tones and variations of mental and physical experience possible in life." Sylvia Plath

I awakened my dreams to weaken my doubts. One day, while updating my playlist yet again, I found a new fitness album on iTunes called Muscle Prodigy. It had a motivational speaker named Jaret Grossman set to rousing music. One Saturday I was running yet another workout marathon. It had been raining for twelve miles or so and my dogs would shake the water off their bodies every few miles. But overall I was feeling good. I was feeling good about my progress, about my energy level, about my speed. My doubts were quiet. I ran with my ball cap on to keep the rain out of my eyes. I had already seen one pluviophilic turtle hauling his heavy home on his moist and mysterious migration. I was listening to this motivating album, when Grossman asked in his focused, baritone voice:

"How big is your appetite for success? Achieving greatness happens when you are willing to do something that will kill you just to make you better."

I thought again about my life regrets. I thought about how much I wanted to be a better physician, about how the residents inspired me and how deeply I wanted to return the favor. I thought about my long ago interest in general surgery. I thought about how satisfying it would be to physically touch and remove someone's disease instead of all the abstract cerebral calisthenics of medical management. It seemed to have fewer diseases caused by patient's choices, and more of simple bad luck. This important separation implicated surgical patients less as perpetrators (or at least accomplices) of their own problems. General surgery residency was certainly something that felt like it would almost kill me, but promised to make me a better physician: increasing skills, facing new difficulties I was afraid of, etcetera. I thought about how I was thirty eight years old. I felt a new kind of doubt; the emotion the German's call "torschlusspanik," which literally translates as "gate-closing panic." It is the fear of diminishing opportunities as we age.

I pushed back. I picked up my pace. I didn't want to listen to doubts. I was running a nameless marathon in the rain just for practice. Wasn't that sufficient evidence that I was willing to do something that might kill me just for the chance it might make me better?

"What about medicine? Are you willing to put in as much work into being a better physician as you are putting in to being a better athlete?"

This was a different voice. This was not a voice of doubt. Whose voice was this?

"What are you even talking about? I'm already a staff physician. I'm even a faculty physician who teaches doctors."

"Yes, you are. But are you willing to do something that might kill you just to make you even better?"

"Yes."

"Then why don't you go back to school and do a general surgery residency?"

I felt my mouth go dry in the rain. Goosebumps stood up on my neck. I had a strange realization that I wasn't dead, or over-the-hill, or washed-up. I was alive. I was still getting better.

I stopped running, but my heart sped up. My dogs blinked up through the rain at me.

It would make for a great adventure, a great book even.

Rain dripped off the brim of my baseball hat as the heavens decanted.

"But what about all that I've learned in family medicine, am I just supposed to abandon my specialty I've spent years learning to master?"

"Have you been as disciplined in studying and in mastering it since you finished residency?"

"Not really."

"Why not use one level of training to prepare you for the next one, the way you are using one race to prepare for the next?"

"Who am I to try to be a surgeon?"

"Who are you to be an Ironman?"

The hair on my arms stood up, the way it does when you have been struck by lightning.

"Is it even possible?"

"You know that it is. You have known physicians who leave family medicine for second residencies to make their lives easier.

Ease is not your path, but because you have prepared for it, your second chance has come."

And so, during my semester of experiments I learned something really, really important: like doubts, dreams are strangely difficult to kill. When we think they were long dead, sometimes they simply wait patiently for us on the roads we take to avoid them.

*Exercise refines your body and your soul and helps you make
the spiritual essence of exercise a part of your very being.
In this way you are able to perfect yourself
and contribute something of value to the world.*
Jigaro Kano, Founder of Judo

*If you want to awaken all of humanity then awaken all of yourself,
if you want to eliminate the suffering in the world, then eliminate
all that is dark and negative in yourself.
Truly, the greatest gift you have to give is
that of your own self-transformation.*
Lao Tzu, Philosopher

MILE 22
Orestes

Anagnorisis: (Greek) (n) in Greek tragedy, the moment of insight when the protagonist recognizes his or some other character's true identity or discovers the nature of his own predicament, which leads to the resolution of the plot.

I thought of all the self-doubts and conversations I had had with myself over the miles and miles. And I was reminded of my favorite story in all of Greek mythology, the myth of Orestes. In this legend Orestes, like me, is born to a family that has a secret.

He was a grandson of Atreus, a man who had angered the gods. Because of this, the gods punished Atreus by placing a curse upon all of his descendants. My own grandfather's heart attacks at a young age had cast a dark shadow over my father and our family's health. Our genetics and our family also seemed to be cursed.

Then, as this curse played out, Orestes' mother, Clytemnestra murdered her husband Orestes' father. So Orestes found himself in an unwinnable situation. According to the Greek codes of honor every son must avenge his father's murder. However, the worst crime a Greek could commit was killing his own mother, the very person who gave him life.

So he was trapped with this decision, stuck between a rock and a hard place.

Orestes agonized over his decision, and then finally did what he felt he had to do: he killed his mother. For committing this abomination, he was punished by the gods. They sent special tormentors, called the Furies, to punish him. The Furies were invisible flying beings that plagued and taunted him. They mocked him and told him he was a terrible person, they woke him up and haunted his dreams. They drove him toward madness.

I completely relate to this part of the story. The voices of my own mind and self-doubts whirl around me, threatening my mental balance and prodding me to do things that don't seem to make sense to people around me.

So Orestes set off on this great quest, wandering the land trying to make things right. He fought monsters, and rescued damsels in distress, but the Furies continued to whirl around him laughing and mocking.

I imagine him getting into the most difficult school he could and slaying test questions and then trying to help sick and dying people who got sick and died anyway. I imagined him doing ultra-endurance sports to try to get rid of these voices.

I imagined him going to some crazy medicine man/cave-dwelling hermit who, though he couldn't see the Furies, believed Orestes. He prescribed him special herbs, potions, pain medicines, anti-depressants, a special diet, and a stretching regimen.

None of it worked. The voices continue whirling around him and shrieking in his mind where no one else could hear.

So, in a moment of wretched hopelessness, Orestes falls down on his knees in the temple of Athena, and begs the gods for mercy. He has done everything he can think of to make things right, and nothing has worked.

The gods heard his prayer, and they grant him his request, and they hold a special trial for him. A pantheon of frowning Greek gods gather for the trial.

In my personalized version of the myth, there is the god-like figure of my father, and the squinting bearded god of medicine, the goddess-like figures of my mother, and my wife, and the god-like figures of my bosses, the god and goddess of my in-laws with their scales in their hands, the god of my church, and the fuzzying god-like memories of my grandparents all staring at me.

Apollo steps forward to be Orestes' lawyer. He makes the case that the Furies should be taken from Orestes, "because it is not his fault." Some of the Greek gods lean forward, tipping their heads. Some raise their eyebrows.

"You see, Orestes didn't ask to be born into this family that is haunted by a curse. He didn't ask to be placed in a no-win situation by his mother's choice to kill his father. It's not Orestes' fault. If anyone is at fault, it is us, the gods. I say we remove the Furies from Orestes."

Well, all the gods lean back and thoughtfully scratch at their beards, except the goddesses, who don't have beards. And they all frown and start nodding their heads slowly in agreement as Apollo's argument builds some momentum.

Then something weird happens.

Orestes stands up and, countering his own lawyer, says, "That is not true. It was I, Orestes who chose to kill my mother. I alone am responsible. Not my grandfather, not my father, not my mother, not the gods. It was my choice."

The gods were astounded. Never had a mortal taken responsibility for all of the bad things in his life instead of blaming the gods! They were so impressed they did something special. They changed the Furies into something called the Eumenides. These were invisible messengers that flew around Orestes and taught him wisdom, gave him counsel, sang quiet songs of praise to him and reminded him that he was a good person.

I love this legend! It teaches how to transform the voices of self-doubt from tormentors into voices of wisdom. In the moment we take complete responsibility for our lives, the very things that cause us agony become transformed into gifts from the gods! The voices of self-doubt that swirl around me are not my curse; they are the greatest gift I have. They are the voices that have taught me wisdom, strength and courage.

It was precisely because of the curse of my grandfather's heart attacks haunting and tormenting my father that he ran. It was partially because of them that I went into medicine. Because my father took responsibility for the curse upon his family my grandfather's curse was transmuted through generations into strength.

My own Furies swirled around my mind and mocked me that I had never excelled in high school sports. It was partially *because* I had only been an average runner in high school that I was still trying to prove myself. When all the star runners had long since quit and put on weight, I had just placed first in my age group in an Ironman. These voices of self-doubt weren't Furies, they were Eumenides!

When I stepped back and considered the other areas of my life that seemed to torment and haunt me the most, I had to ponder what wisdom they too were trying to teach me. I thought about the patients who puzzled and baffled me. Many times I saw them through the lens of my own self-doubts. Or, as Anais Nin once said, "We don't see things as they are, we see them as we are." As I began to see myself more clearly, I began to see them more clearly. My patients were not there to torment me or stump me, or to make me feel foolish. They were in my life to teach me wisdom and compassion. They stretched and strengthened my own capacity to love.

Slowly I learned to love them because they were also haunted by sometimes invisible tormentors that told them they were unlovable. Some patients were tormented by invisible back pains whose origins I could neither detect with physical examination nor with an MRI scanner. They were invisible, but I believed the pain was there. Some people were tormented by their weight and the voices in their minds that said they were unattractive and unlovable. Some told me of their PTSD from their deployments, and how it haunted them. If I believed they could handle it, I asked these patients if they ever thought of their illnesses as a gift. What had they learned from their illnesses?

Like many of my patients, my Furies told me my body was not attractive. I am, and have always been skinny. The Furies told me this also meant that I was weak and unappealing. I lost myself in the whole semester of experiments, but I found myself there too. It took months of painful experiments to try to determine what was the truth about the human body, and where were the lies I had been fed? What was real life and what was photoshopped magazine fantasy? When I really exercised I learned I was hungry all the time. And I ate until I was stuffed. When I was starving my gut was flat. When I had eaten as much as I could hold, my gut stuck out. That was real, and it stopped bothering me.

I saw a quote that read, "I don't have a tattoo for the same reason that you don't put a bumper sticker on a Ferrari." I liked the self-confidence of this quote, but I had to ask myself if I really considered my body a Ferrari? Or did I think of it as an old *hand me down* sedan?

My friend Sowell once told me she wanted to buy a bikini.

"Don't you think that bikinis are distracting to the guys?"

She looked at me and said, "If guys have a problem with looking at women's bodies that is their problem. They better get themselves under control. My problem is I've been told not to like my own body, like I have to hide it or I'll be teased for it not looking perfect. My problem is I am trying to love how my own body looks, and to not feel ashamed and like I'm not allowed to look beautiful. It's not about making other people admire my body; it's about earning my own admiration."

Prior to this semester, when I looked at myself in the mirror, I didn't really like what I saw. So, I forced myself to run with my shirt off. Part of this was to minimize sweating, but part of it was to desensitize myself to my overly sensitive self-criticisms of my own body. Jayne Cox once said, "It is easier to wake up early and work out than it is to look in the mirror each day and not like what you see." The more I ran the more I loved my body. Not because it's perfect, but because with every mile it showed me I was physically and mentally capable of more than I had believed possible. As I exercised and ate better and took better care of myself, my relationship with my own body changed. I learned to respect, embrace and love my body because it is an amazing gift from God; the only body I have. Gradually, instead of filling me with embarrassment, it filled me with a sense of awe.

Old habits die hard, and sometimes I still look at my body and find things to pick at. And then I remind myself I had made my own body as epic as humanly possible. In return it had made me an ultramarathoner and prepared me to do an event whose name had struck awe in me my entire life. I say to myself, "though imperfect, that is what the body of an Ironman looks like," and I quiet the criticisms. I like how I look in the mirror. I like who I am becoming, in part because I have fought so hard to become this me. At the end of it all, there were ten pounds less of me on the earth. All my worries and emotions and love had to fit into a smaller, tighter version of myself, making them all the more concentrated.

Finally, my Furies laughed at me and told me I was not a good physician. They cackled and reminded me of my struggles during my residency. They told me that I wasn't good enough or smart enough. Rather than torment me, I let the space between where I was and where I wanted to be inspire me. I didn't want to ignore, or to silence my self-doubts, I wanted to listen to them, to keep track of them, and to learn from them. I wanted to domesticate my doubts. I began the application process to go back to residency, to put myself through another endurance event, to become a better version of myself and closer to the me I want to be.

There is a Zen proverb that says, "Where there is great doubt, there will be great awakening; small doubt, small awakening; no doubt: no awakening." Perhaps my great doubts were there to wake me up and teach me great things....

I wasn't expecting it, but training for the semester of endurance experiments helped me remember and become the person I wanted to become when I was a little kid. It helped me become the kind of person the younger me would have liked to meet. It helped me to remember who I am, and the legacy I wanted to leave for my children. It showed me a path out of my father's shadow. It even helped me to realize it wasn't really his shadow I was trying to escape anyway. It was my own. It was the shadows of my doubts. Ironically, I discovered my strength was born out of my relationship with these doubts. I used to believe that athletes were individuals who were super self-confident, to the point of braggadocio. But I now believe self-doubt can be as powerful a fuel as self-confidence. The fear of not being good enough can fuel us to try to become better. My doubts are valuable to me because they force me to learn, even when I don't want to.

It is the possibility of having a dream come true
that makes life interesting.
Paulo Coelho, Author

Weakness will not be in my heart.
I will look to my comrades,
to those who brought me into this world,
and those who have trained me,
and I will draw strength from them.
John Flowers, Football Coach

MILE 23
MY OLD MAN AND THE
IRONMAN

Resfeber (Swedish) (n): The restless race of the traveler's heart before the journey begins, when anxiety and anticipation are tangled together, a "travel fever" that can manifest as an illness.

I don't know if it was because I am a wounded worrier, but part of me was genuinely afraid this race might kill me. I was afraid my wife and I might get in an accident on the long drive to Texas. I was afraid because 2.4 miles was farther than I had ever swam. I might drown far from help out in the middle of the lake. I was afraid the dark gray wet suit would make it even harder to find my body. I imagined it submerged for days being nibbled on by fish until it bloated up and floated to the surface. I was afraid that I would be hit by a car while riding the bike portion, or have a terrible crash. I was afraid that during the run I might put my heart under so much strain that I would have a heart attack. I was afraid I would overcompensate for the projected ninety degree Texas heat and drink too much water and develop hyponatremia, or maybe not drink enough and get dehydrated. I was afraid the exertion would be so great my muscles would break down and that I would develop rhabdomyolysis.

I smiled—my doubts were still there. They were such stalwart company!

My bike was seventeen years old. My father rode his first bike for twenty-six years. I heard once that mid-life crises weren't necessarily bad things; sometimes they happen because someone has delayed gratification for so long they had reached a tipping point and finally felt they had earned something nice. When some people reach this tipping point they stereotypically buy sports cars. In keeping with his spirit, when my father reached this point, he splurged and finally allowed himself to buy a brand new, lightweight, beautiful fourteen speed bicycle. But the sheer elegance of his new bike created a certain degree of guilt. Having inherited his fiscal conservatism, I also struggled with guilty feelings over nice things. In my own way, I was hoping that if I completed an Ironman I would finally have earned the right to buy a new bike. Though I had to admit the strangeness of my logic as I would most benefit from a new bike during the race...

My father's buyer's remorse and my own delayer's dissatisfaction aligned perfectly: just before the Ironman my dad offered me to use his bike. Now, he could feel better because such a gorgeous purchase could be purified through charitable association, and I could enjoy the benefit of a newer bike without the cost. My dad was keeping his part of our pact: he was lending his support to help me.

As the "full" triathlon would be in Texas, Katie and I drove there over two days. My parents drove down from Kansas, and we met at their hotel on the afternoon prior to the race. My dad brought his bike for me to size up. Because my bike shoes were a size bigger than his, we had to somehow switch pedals. But the pedals on his bike could not be removed. I yanked and pulled in vain on the wrench, but it was like trying to remove Excalibur. Finally my dad discovered that we could just switch the cleats on our bike shoes.

Obstacle conquered.

We made a couple other adjustments to the aerobars, and added my extra water bottle cages. My dad told me that on his last hundred mile race his bike was not the fastest at climbing, but "it screams down hills." I wondered if this was a comment about how his gear cogs were set up, but comparing it to my own bike, they were the same. Remembering my flat at the last race, I made sure I had both a spare inner tube, and my own CO_2 canisters. My dad gave me his plain white cycling jersey. No silly pseudo-sponsors, just a plain pragmatic color to minimize absorption of the Texas heat. I loved it because my father's racing shirts had always been magic to me. White was the color of a ghost. And besides, I was the sponsor of my own dreams.

Seeing us fiddling with the bikes, a father and son who were staying at the same hotel came over and introduced themselves. They said that they were going to be doing the half distance the next day at the same time and asked what course I would be doing. I told them I was going to try to do the full. As soon as the words were out of my mouth, a quote from Yoda came to my mind, "Do or do not, there is no try." I realized by saying the word "try" I was creating a hedge, perhaps to acknowledge uncertainty, and perhaps to show humility, but it risked weakening me. The word risked creating enough psychological wiggle room, that it might give me room to quit. So I corrected myself and said, "I will do the full Ironman distance tomorrow."

We went to the pre-race meeting, were I learned there were more than two hundred people signed up for the half distance, and fourty-five people signed up for the full. People dropped their breathtaking bikes off at the transition area. It looked like a parking lot for bike Ferraris. Many of these bikes cost more than my car. As I looked at their featherweight frames that had been perfected in wind tunnels, I felt both envy and pity. It is possible to buy some speed, but the majority of it can only be bought with long, difficult practice to train the engine that powers it. I knew there were some imposters present who hoped their bikes would compensate for their lack of preparation. But I also knew some of these people had earned their bikes, and they were the ones who intimidated me because they were impossible to discern. Only the miles would tease them apart.

My father approached me with a serious expression."It looks like it is against the rules to have a pacer. I don't want you to do the whole race only to get disqualified for running the last thirteen miles with me," he said.

"I don't want to either. I've been training almost half a year to get here."

"But at the same time," he said, "I've been training to be able to run with you, and I was really looking forward to it."

"I was too dad. You were part of my race strategy."

I approached one of the race organizers and asked about pacers.

"Well, technically they are against the rules, but sometimes someone has one of their kids or someone who wants to run a little bit with them."

"Yeah," I said, "father-son kinds of things are nice memories."

"I can't authorize it because of the rules," he said, with a sparkle in his eyes, "but it is a big course, and even when I try, I can't always see everything that happens out there." He cleared his throat.

Obstacle conquered.

The night before, as usual, I couldn't sleep. I kept waking up thinking about all the million little pieces I needed to coordinate: the GU gels, fear that I would sleep in and miss the start; remembering to apply my number tattoos, and remember safety pins for my bib number. I ran the race in my mind, visualizing the 2.4 mile swim, the 112 mile bike ride and then the marathon. My father wanted to run the second half of the marathon with me, and I imagined reaching him, exhausted but knowing with a certainty that if I could reach him I would make it the rest of the way. Out of curiosity, I looked at the clock. It was midnight. I stretched my body, and everything felt rested and strong. I had no aching injuries, no areas of soreness. But I didn't feel restless either; just good and ready. My taper had been better this time. I had finally figured it out.

When my alarm finally sounded, I was deep asleep. I shrugged off the grogginess and felt my heartbeat speed up. One part of me said this was nervousness; the other part corrected me for my poor word choice. Sometimes the words we use to speak to ourselves have unintended consequences. Taking a page out of the UFC Hall of Famer, Randy Couture's book of tricks, I corrected myself: I did not feel *nervous*; I felt "excitement."

I got ready, taking a quick shower, putting in my contact lenses, and slathering on the sunscreen to both help with the later events, and also help me slide into the wetsuit. I would burn over 11,000 calories during the race, but my stomach was nervous. For breakfast, I ate a banana (100 calories) and a package of Oreos (280 calories). I told myself I'd make up the rest on the bike...

At the transition area, the excitement was palpable. I did not want the adrenaline to sap my strength, and leave me feeling hollowed out, so I tried to busy myself with lots of little jobs. I kept feeling the urge to pee, so I knew the adrenaline was revving my sympathetic fight or flight system up. I made it to the port-a-potty (barefoot, ugh) one last time before walking down to the lake. Some people were swimming a practice lap to warm up. Those doing the full Ironman distance were given dark blue swim caps, and those doing the half were given light blue. I looked around at the sea of light blue caps and felt strangely apart. My wife, mother and father stood just to the side of the lake.

While we were waiting for the final minutes to tick down, my wife waved me over, and showed me a text message she had just received from our son. It said, "Tell dad that I love him."

The sky was dark, but just starting to lighten. There were clouds overhead. I prayed they would last. I noticed other swimmers rolling up their wetsuit zipper strings and carefully securing the small bundle under the Velcro flap at their necks. Remembering how it had distracted me at the last race when it touched my arm, I did this too. When the swim began, the crowd was so dense I knew we would be bumping into each other. I had seventeen hours to finish, so a couple extra seconds that risked a kick to the face were not worth it to me. I eased into the crowd where there was room, and then worked on finding my pace.

The visibility in the clear water was excellent. Even in the dim light I could see at least six feet below me. As my arms fell into their rhythm of reaching, catching, pulling, I remembered to kick from my hips and keep my knees fairly straight. As I thought about why this water was so clear, and the "certified pristine" waters back at Florida had been so murky, I remembered that anywhere there is beautiful clear water; it is a sign that there is little nutrition in the surrounding soil to drain into the water. I thought about my little breakfast and smiled.

With each breath I swam between a world of brightening shoreline, and a world of silent wetness. As the sky brightened enormous water plants bloomed into view below me extending even further into darkness. Though their shapes were alien to me, I was grateful the water clarity allowed me to see them so I wasn't reaching my hand down into an invisible surprise. I was also grateful there weren't any alligators.

The average Ironman swim took 120 minutes. The month before I had swum the half distance in thirty-nine minutes, but I wasn't sure if I could, or should, hold that pace. After all, I had only been swimming regularly for two months, and I had a long ways to go. When I rounded the first lap, I was right at forty minutes. During the second lap, I worked to not zig-zag too much. I swam ten strokes of freestyle, then five strokes of breaststroke. This let me both re-orient myself and catch my breath. I came out of the water at exactly eighty minutes; better than average, and better than I had hoped. I believe this happened because I was so fresh and rested. I had worked to use my arms and just wear them completely out. But to keep my legs up I had also tried to "swim downhill," which required me to kick them. I still struggled with breathing on both sides.

At the transition point I pulled on my padded bike shorts, and my cargo bike shorts over those. I sat down and struggled into my trusty toe socks. I put on another layer of sun screen, my GPS watch, helmet, and sunglasses. My phone was clipped to the handlebars this time so my family could track me, and I could call for help if needed. Then I ratcheted my bike shoes on and click-stepped my father's bike out of the transition area. I could have been faster on the transition, but I tried to be smooth and deliberate so I didn't miss anything. Somewhere in the transition, the banana came out of the back of my cycling shirt, and I sat on it, which was gross.

The bike section began with a hill that stretched up for a mile. I relaxed and familiarized myself with my dad's gear shifters. With a push of the shifter, the chain snapped crisply to the next gear. It was like a digital shifter, compared to my old analog shifters I had to tease into just the right thread. Many books warn athletes to never try anything new on a race they haven't fully vetted during practice. I knew that riding on my father's bike presented some potential risks: was the seat going to be putting pressure on the same areas I had conditioned to pressure? Was the handlebar angle going to strain different back muscles?

Once I got to the top of the first hill, I found my father's assessment of his bike's speed on downhills was correct: I flew down the hill. Training in Florida, I did not have many hills, and none could prepare me for all of these. The races and the hills are certainly bigger in Texas. Initially I was worried about them, but I found that if I shifted to the easiest "granny gear" and stood up to climb I actually passed more people on the uphills than I did on the downhills. Standing up had several advantages: first, it used completely different muscles, as it was much closer to running than to biking, so it actually felt like it gave my muscles a break. Second, it got me off the seat, and gave my tiring bottom a break too. Even when it burned and my breaths started really huffing on the uphills, I knew I would recover quickly on the downhills.

As the sun rose, the clouds stuck around protecting and encouraging me to get moving while the weather was cool. From the top of each hill, I looked for cyclists ahead of me. Thankfully, the bike and the run portion shared routes with the half distance athletes. The only difference was we would do each route twice. So, though they had had a shorter swim, I soon found myself catching competitors and reeling them in. Spectators lined the early parts of the course, and one of them held up a sign that said, "Trust Your Training."

I covered the first fifty miles in a little over three hours. If I had been that fast on the half Ironman the previous month, I would have been a real contender. I felt strong, and I felt confident. Then, in the middle of yet another hill, the front gear-shifter stopped working, converting the fourteen speed bike into a seven speed. I dearly missed the lowest gears on those hills.

No one had passed me yet, but suddenly, everyone around me was finishing their bike portion, and there were only a few of us returning for a second lap. The hills seemed larger, and the headwind seemed stronger with no one around to hunt down. Having people around to race brought a curious sense of both competition, and camaraderie. When I compete, I do not do it to hurt or defeat anyone. I do it to measure myself. I need external people to act as measuring sticks for my own soul, my own determination, my own strength. I recognize they are inherently elastic measuring sticks, but they were the best I had. Around mile sixty I began sparing with another rider. He passed me while

I was drinking some water, and I passed him again later when he was stopping to hug his wife.

Wildflowers grew along much of the course. Mile after mile of dark red Indian Paintbrushes reminded me of my grandfather who had told me their name when I was a boy. Their red contrasted with blue bells, the state flower of Texas, and some sort of bright yellow flower. Despite their sheer numbers, between the wind and my speed I could not smell them. My dogs would have been disappointed in me. And though they certainly brightened the view, they also brought their own hazards.

On one long downhill, where I was going over thirty miles an hour, a bumblebee hit me in the lower lip, and brought tears to my eyes. Also along the road were multiple sun-bleached carcasses from road kill: a deer, a small wild pig, a couple of dogs, and some unidentifiable smaller animals. There were even some vultures on one part of the course waiting for us to pass so they could get back to work on an armadillo. It made me smile to think the cartoon depictions of Texas were proving to be surprisingly accurate. But smiling made my lower lip hurt, and I didn't want any bugs to hit me in the teeth, so I stopped.

An ambulance wailed passed me. Someone must have crashed…

Nutrition was a sport within the sport. In training I had learned to recognize that my mood frequently signaled when I was hungry. I had felt good for much of the course, but I could feel annoying little thoughts starting to rise up and bloom like these wild flowers. I ate cheesy crackers. I ate a bag of gum drops. I ate a power bar. I drank Gatorade with an extra salt packet added. Each of these had its own disadvantages and my gut began arguing with me. When I passed my cheering family around mile thirty-five I asked for a banana. They passed me in the minivan and Katie got out. I could see she had a banana in her hand. As I approached, she peeled the banana, wanting to help. Going twenty miles an hour the wet, peeled banana slipped into and then right out of my hand.

Then, at mile seventy, just a couple of miles out of the aid station where I had picked up a water bottle, the road became extremely bumpy. I felt like I was about to rattle my teeth out of my head, and wondered if it was because this new water bottle wasn't sitting snuggly in the bottle cage. As I fiddled with it, I realized this much vibration could not be from the water bottle, and I looked down.

I had a flat tire and was riding on the metal rim. I had replaced the tires on my bike to a pair that was more puncture resistant, but I had forgotten when I switched to my father's bike.

I pulled over and called my wife to see if they could help me. They reported they had gone into town to buy some food, so they were nowhere near-by. They called my dad, who they had dropped off at the next intersection, about ten miles away. I started changing the flat. The tire itself was pretty worn, my father loved to put miles on his bike. I had really dinged up the rim by riding about a hundred yards on it. I took the tire off and pulled the inner tube out, then ran my finger around the entire inner perimeter of the tire, searching for thorns or anything sharp that might have punctured through. Not finding anything, I put in my single spare tube, and attached my single CO_2 canister. The tire inflated, but I had not completely tucked the tire into the rim on one area, so it ballooned out in that area. I had to deflate it a little to tuck the tire back into the rim. When I tried to re-inflate it, using the remainder of the CO_2 canister, it only filled partway. It was serviceable, but not rigid. My dad called and told me he had sent a sag wagon my direction to help with the flat.

I started riding, and about two miles later an SUV with a bike on the back caught up to me. The man asked if I needed help. Knowing that CO_2 leaks out of tires faster than normal air because the molecules are smaller, I asked if he had a pump. He did, so I pulled over and he pumped my bike up to a full hundred pounds of pressure. He told me he had been racing, but he had crashed, and blew out his tire and bent his rim—it was beyond repair. I noticed the road rash on his shoulder, leg and face.

"If all my training is done, I'm at least going to do something good with my day."

I thanked him and took off, hoping to catch everyone who had passed me. He waved good-bye and disappeared down the road. Three miles later, my back tire made a loud pop, and went flat again. I had no more spares, and no more CO_2.

For a split second, I felt fear that I might not be able to finish this race. I imagined all the months of training, and all the hopes I had had. I was tired, but I still had energy, I knew I could keep moving, but I couldn't run in these rigid bike shoes, and I was only at mile seventy-two of the 112 miles of the bike course. Part of me wanted to feel relief, like I had gotten out of something really painful through no fault of my own. No one would fault me. And it would get me out of running a marathon when I was already feeling tired. But I did not feel relief, I wanted to keep going. I also worried about how much time I was losing, as there was a time cut-off to finish the bike portion. If I did not make the 5:30pm cut-off, then I would be disqualified.

So this was what it felt like when a dream dies.

I called my dad again and told him what happened. He said he would send another vehicle my way. I waited in the shade of a mesquite tree, and enjoyed the chance to stretch my legs. They had started to get tired, and this little break actually lifted my spirit before the fatigue had set in too deeply. It also gave me a chance to eat something and drink some more while my stomach was holding still.

The second vehicle arrived and the man was from one of the local bike shops. He looked through his tools for a file to see if he could smooth down the jagged edges of the rim. Not finding a file, he changed the tube and gave me a brand new high quality tire as well. I thanked him and got back on the road.

The break felt good, but the whole ordeal had set me back almost forty minutes, five people had passed me, and now I was fighting headwinds up hills for miles. My left big toe went numb from pushing against the inflexible cycling shoes. I just wanted to be able to bend my foot. My upper back started cramping from leaning forward on the bike, and my bottom hurt from sitting for so long. None of these were unexpected, I had experienced them all during my long training rides, but they still hurt and nagged.

I pedaled on and on, but I only caught three of the people who passed me before the bike was over. One hundred and twelve miles.

The marathon loomed before me. I had been intentionally ignoring it, pushing thoughts of it away.

"You're exhausted, and now you have to run a marathon."

"I have run many marathons before."

"Not anytime recently. In fact, you haven't run one in over two months, you've just been doing those twenty-two mile runs to work where you really only run eleven miles each way with a huge break in the middle while you sit at your desk all day. Even your long runs on Saturday you only ran twelve! "

"All those miles of bike training have some fitness overlap with my legs, heart and lungs."

"But, your longest ride was only a hundred miles, and they were much flatter than this."

For a single moment, I imagined returning home and telling my kids I had quit. The thought of leaving them with that legacy, and that example stirred me. I resolved to run my body into the ground before I would quit. I knew my body would heal, I knew I would recover from whatever damage I might do. I took a deep breath.

Your legs are not giving out. Your head is giving up. Keep going.

"You know you aren't going to break the record, no one even cares about people who finish in the middle of the pack."

I am not going to stop just because I am tired. I will stop when I am done.

"Your legs are already done."

I had planned an ambush for this argument.

"I know I can run a half marathon. If I can do that, then I can reach my dad. If I can reach my dad, his strength will get me through the second half. If I can reach my dad, I can finish."

I knew I could reach him. The race was both external to me, but also inside my own head. Over all the preceding events, and months of training I had not only conditioned my body, but also my mind and my beliefs. Coach Flowers said, "I have trained my mind, and my body will follow." What I discovered was I had had to train my body for my mind to follow. I trusted my training, but I also doubted my training. My mind never quite trusted my body, and vice versa. Like any relationship the trust had been built gradually, tentatively, cautiously. My mental confidence was proportional to my physical preparation.

I pulled into the transition area. I only had to change my shoes, and swap my bike helmet for a ball cap to keep the sun off my head. The sun was still up, so I applied another dose of sunscreen, being careful to avoid putting any on my forehead so it wouldn't get carried by my sweat down into my eyes, especially while I was wearing contacts. I had lost much of the pressure to be fast. As I walked out of the fenced area I ate a banana on a stomach that wasn't competing with my thighs for blood. The marathon consisted of running the half marathon course out and back along the shoulder of a freeway, and then doing it again. It ended at the local hospital's parking lot. This seemed ominous and familiar at the same time.

I forgot how relaxing it felt to run after biking! My feet felt so good to actually be able to move and bend. My upper back had cramped from leaning forward on the bike, and as I swung my arms with each stride, the cramps dissolved. My legs, instead of being tired, felt relieved to be using different muscles, to be standing up instead of sitting on that bike seat. The cramp in my left thigh vanished. I hadn't appreciated how nice it would feel simply to stand upright. I hadn't anticipated that running would feel really, really good.

The last two people I had passed on the bike had passed me again in the transition area. I started after them, grimly telling myself I would reel them in. I thought a firm and competitive spirit would be the final font of strength.

Then something unexpected happened. As I approached I saw them. They were no longer helmeted colors, whose eyes were buried under sunglasses. They were tired and suffering like me and they were pressing forward anyway. To pass them I would have to hear their footsteps and breathing. I didn't want my passing them to be a source of discouragement to them. I wanted them to finish. My sense of competition was replaced by a sense of admiration and compassion. The race itself had changed at the transition area. Somehow at the transition area, the race itself had transitioned from a competition to a cooperative event.

The first person I caught was a woman in a green singlet. She was running with a man who had an Ironman tattoo on the back of his right thigh. I ran along with them briefly, trying to figure out what to say, but my thoughts wouldn't organize. They were not speaking. When they stopped to walk the uphill part of the first hill, I kept moving because I felt awkward.

The second runner was running alone. As I approached him, I could see we were going about the same speed. I tried to say something encouraging as I approached.

"Those clouds have really been kind to us today."

He looked at the sky we were running toward. The sun was still behind some clouds. He made a noise that sounded thankful.

We started talking as we ran. I was grateful for the company, and he seemed to be also. His name was Harish, and this was also his first full Ironman distance triathlon. When I asked why he was doing this race, he said he was going to be entering a training program with eighty-hour work weeks for five years so he didn't know if he would have time to do something like this for a while. Like me, he had felt the time pressure of doing it now, or never, and had harnessed the pressure to do it. Already knowing the answer, I asked him what kind of a training program has you work eighty-hour weeks for five years.

"I'm a medical student," he said, "and I just got accepted into a general surgery residency."

I smiled to myself and laughed inwardly at the God's sense of humor, especially when He explains His own jokes.

The hills somehow seemed even larger when we were jogging compared to when we had ridden them, and there were some pretty lonely stretches of road. There were aid tables every couple of miles, and the aid workers offered drinks and encouragement. As we ran along, my family leapfrogged us along the way in their vehicle, taking pictures and giving encouragement. When we approached another runner, we invited them to run along with us. We knew how lonely it was with only tired thoughts for company. We wanted everyone to finish.

For a little while another runner, Todd joined us. It was also his first ironman distance. He told us he had lost over a hundred pounds getting in shape for this. I was so impressed with him, and thought about how it would feel to go from sitting on a couch to finishing an Ironman. What an inspirational story and legacy!

The fatigue caught up with us, and eventually we began walking the uphills, and only running the downhills and flats. We took turns picking out areas ahead where we would walk, and were we would resume running.

"That sign?"

"Okay."

"Where the pavement changes colors?"

"Sounds good."

We spoke about medicine, about obesity. We looked at the flowers. After a few miles, Todd kept walking when we agreed to run at the next post. Slowly he dropped behind. Harish and I kept going. Nausea set in after a while, and though we stopped at the food tables and tried to find something that our stomachs would accept, eating was as forced as running. I realized that I hadn't peed for over three hours. I drank at every food table, trying to get rehydrated, but then became worried that I wasn't replacing enough salt and would develop hyponatremia. My mind started slipping, and wondered what hyponatremia would feel like. Five slow miles later I finally started peeing again.

My legs were exhausted. My mind instantly interpreted this as a sure sign of rhabdomyolysis. My imagination flipped though memories of patients with "rhabdo" I had admitted over the years. The treatment was admission to a hospital with IV fluid to protect the kidneys as the muscle proteins could cause kidney failure. I was okay with it if it happened. In that state of mind, kidney failure was an acceptable outcome.

We made it halfway, and my dad joined us. He had been watching all day, itching to participate. We showed him how we walked the uphills and picked a spot to start running again. The food tables gave us headlamps. The sun set slowly, but I didn't notice the color because I was looking down at the pavement.

My lungs ached, feeling stretched from breathing so deeply for so long. I could feel my heartbeat increase going up the hills. I wondered if I could have a heart attack if I didn't have a blockage. Could I have one just from exertion? I did have substernal chest pain, which was worse when we started running again and relieved by rest. I imagined the residents presenting my symptoms to me. I would be admitted to a hospital and get blood drawn every eight hours looking for cardiac enzyme elevations, and having EKGs. In the morning I would have an exercise stress test and run on a treadmill. The idea of running on a treadmill to rule out my exercise-induced chest pain made me smile. I didn't think I should stop running just because I was having typical angina symptoms.

I thought about my wife and kids. Running myself to death while doing a monster triathlon would be a fine way to die. I would be okay with that. But doing so would probably scar my wife and kids and make them afraid of running. I was not okay with that.

An ambulance raced passed us. We later learned it was picking up Todd.

Another runner caught up to us. "I could see your lights, and I've been trying up to catch you."

I wished I had my music to listen to. I asked if our little band wanted to sing a cadence. My dad said, "Sure." Harish said he would try. During my runs I had noticed that one of my favorite poems could be sung as a cadence as I ran.

"Okay, I'll sing first, and you guys echo it."

"Okay."

I took a deep breath. It hurt my lungs. I imagined an old rubber band that was stretched and wouldn't go back to its original shape.

Out of the dark that covers me.

They echoed me after each line, matching our footsteps to the beat.

Black as the pit from pole to pole,
I thank whatever gods may be

For my unconquerable soul.

Only my father and Harish echoed the last line. Two voices echoing my own tired voice.

In the fell clutch of circumstance
I have not winced nor cried aloud.
Under the bludgeonings of chance
My head is bloody, but unbowed.

One of the four headlight circles stopped moving to the beat and slowly drifted behind us as we sang and trotted along.

Beyond this place of wrath and tears
Looms but the Horror of the shade
And yet the menace of the years
Finds and shall find me unafraid.

It matters not how strait the gait,
How charged with punishments the scroll,
I am the master of my fate,
I am the captain of my soul.

We shuffled along. The other runner was walking. My father looked back.

"I'm going to stay with him. No one should be alone out here in the dark." I imagined him thinking about the ambulance and wondering what had happened to Todd.

I looked at Harish. "What a day."

"We got this," he said, "that black line?"

I grunted, and we started shuffling again when we reached it. My legs were shot. It was an interesting feeling. When my legs are really exhausted, they don't swing through a long arc, but rather take small shuffling steps. We could see the lights from the hospital parking lot shining up against the dark sky, just over the next hills.

"I think these are the last hills, the last few miles."

"Let's do it."

Harish began running. I didn't know if I had anything left, but I clung to his instruction. Harish stretched out his legs. I wasn't sure I could do it, but he was going to leave everything out there. I surrendered to his will and we ran the final hills.

We ran to the finish line. I thought about how this was the final finish line of this semester. I was ready to be weakened by it. Harish strode across the line one stride before me, and we came to a halt.

Katie took pictures, and then hugged me the way you would hug a large, smelly, wet object, like a catfish. I was pretty disgusting. When I felt the warmth of her hug, I felt some of my broken pieces sticking back together.

The words of F. Scott Fitzgerald came to mind "I don't ask you to love me always like this, but I ask you to remember. Somewhere inside of me there will always be the person I am tonight."

The journey is part of the experience—
an expression of the seriousness of one's intent.
One doesn't take a train to Mecca.
Anthony Bourdain, Traveler

I soon realized that no journey carries one far unless,
as it extends into the world around us,
it goes an equal distance into the world within.
Lillian Smith, Writer

MILE 24
Running ~~from~~ with God

Avra Kehdabra: (Aramaic), Abracadabra (English). literally, "I will create as I speak."

When I looked up the race results the next day, I discovered that in an Ironman distance triathlon, I had placed eleventh overall. One footstep ahead of me, and completely deserving it, Harish placed tenth.

I looked at my age division. I had placed first!

A familiar voice told me that it didn't count, that it wasn't a real Ironman brand, and that there weren't even very many people in my age group who had survived to cross the finish line. My doubts liked to use my sanity for their scratching post.

I ignored them.

I was in too much awe. I felt like I had discovered how a really difficult magic trick was done. Until I knew the secret of this "sleight of foot," my imagination had filled in the blanks, distorting and magnifying things out of proportion. One of the things my imagination "mis-underestimated" was how long it would take to recover. The idea of being broken for weeks had intimidated me. In one of the final experiments, I learned that if I was in proper shape to complete these events, then my body was also conditioned to recover from them. I was tired the next day, but surprisingly not that sore. It was weird.

The finisher's shirt was the same generic one given to the people who competed in all of the different triathlon distances that weekend. I didn't really like it. Sometimes, just as you just have to design your own life, you just have to design your own shirt. So I did. I kept one for myself, then gave one to my wife, my son and daughter, and my father. I smiled to myself; I was giving my dad a magic race shirt. "Ironman" is printed on the front. On the back it reads, "Pain is inevitable, Suffering is Optional." The right sleeve said, "Stronger than my excuses," to acknowledge the doubting devils who had been such stalwart company on that shoulder for all those hours and miles. The left sleeve said, "Team Stephensen," to acknowledge the angels on my left shoulder. None of us can achieve our major goals alone. We need people's help. I needed Katie, my Dad, and my kids' support. I needed David's wet suit, and Balderston's swim lessons, and Olshefski's tips, and the old aerobars that Thai sold me for ten bucks. Salguero supported me when she gave me a lift to our nursing home rounds on a day I ran to work, etcetera, etcetera.

But the most significant member of that team of supporters had been God. I don't know all the reasons there was something inside of me that felt called to do this semester of experiments. I had no idea the number of things I would learn, or how it would change me. But studying pain and suffering intimately for such lengthy periods reconfigured my understanding of God and medicine, including what I should do with my medical career going forward.

Just as I had intentionally caused difficulty for myself, some people certainly bring the suffering of their medical problems on themselves. Some ailments were simply physical manifestations of internal struggles: people take up smoking to quiet their social self-consciousness, until their lung cancer causes them a new sense of loneliness; obese patients who ate their anxious thoughts until their mental worries were replaced with physical ones as their backs and knees groaned under the weight of their swollen bodies. Their hurts just changed form, but continued to haunt them. But some people just had horrible, unfair, unasked for bad luck.

Medicine shook my faith in God with the ancient and pitiless question: "if there is a loving God, why is there so much suffering in the world?"

There was part of me that shook my fist at the heavens for the terrible things some people had to go through. Why did my patient have to have cystic fibrosis? He did nothing to deserve it. Why had my sister's son Orion died? Why did the patient I'd screened for breast cancer get it anyway and die? I didn't understand. In my prayers for my patients I asked God, and I got no answer. He seemed so far away, and so busy. And so I secretly got mad at Him. I decided to give Him the silent treatment, and I stopped kneeling down and praying at night. I stopped praying for my patients, and I stopped praying for help.

That was when I fell into addiction; turning to something else to distract my mind from my anxious, worrying thoughts. And my life caved in.

Then, while reading Patrick Carne's book on addiction recovery he had a page filled with adjectives with the instructions to "Circle the six words that best describe how you understand God or your Higher Power." I looked at them.

"Judgmental," Warm," "Arbitrary," "Terrifying," "Loving," "Distant," "Judgmental," "Caring," "Strict," "Absent," etcetera.

I started circling the ones I felt: "Powerful," "Distant," and "Caring."

The next page asked, "Are there any correlations between the adjectives that describe your Higher Power and the descriptions of the caregivers in your life?"

I re-read the list I had circled, thinking of my dad.

"All of them," I realized.

It then suggested that if the God of my understanding was not powerful enough to help me, I probably needed a new God. This was probably intended as a provocative statement, and it did make me think. If God created me with a certain intentionality, then I should probably return the favor. I thought about what kind of a God I needed. I gave him a new name. I stopped calling him Heavenly Father, and started calling him God. I needed a God who cared about suffering. I needed a God who was strong enough to hold me together and take my pain when I was overwhelmed so that I didn't pass it on, but also so I didn't implode into addiction anymore.

Tyler Knott Gregson put it perfectly: "Sometimes," he said while gripping tight the fabric of his own pant leg, "you run out of tears long before you run out of hurt."

To improve my understanding of God, I   needed a better explanation for what suffering was all about, and why bad things happened to good people. The relationship between God and suffering was critical.

It was precisely when I was stuck and confused by these questions that I came across a story by an Islamic teacher that helped give me the new understanding I was looking for. In the story there was a young man at the religious school who asked his Imam the same question that haunted me. "If there is a God, why is there so much suffering in the world, why doesn't God do something?"

The Imam looked at his student.

"He did do something about the suffering that is all around us," he said, smiling "God sent you."

When I read this, it hit me like an arrow had gone straight through my hard and confused heart. I thought of all the patients I had seen, all their pains and sores, and lab results, all their tears, and worries, and miscarriages, and questions I couldn't answer. I was there to help do something about the suffering.

Of all my experiments and discoveries during the semester of explorations the most surprising was to discover that my God does not live in a comfortable, effortless place called Heaven: He lives in the places of pain. He lives with those who are hurting, and wounded. He lives in long runs. This became especially important when I became uncomfortable and when my body hurt. Fitness always has a certain baseline discomfort, both while training, and while recovering. Perhaps this is a just another trait of my father I am projecting on to my understanding of God, but I needed a God who loves fitness. I believe exercise and taking good care of our bodies shows respect to the God who gave them to us in the first place. I believe the pain of physical exercise is just spiritual training through other means because it teaches us about suffering.

Even before the semester began I had been a student of pain and suffering. One thing I had learned was that not all pain is significant. Sometimes it is only pain. Once, while running the eleven miles to work, I hurt my left hamstring around mile four. I thought of quitting, or calling my wife to come get me. But then I realized that I was already hurt, so I might as well get something out of it. I kept running.

Spending so much time in my own company, and in my own misery, I developed a complex interior, and an "interiority complex." I decided to become an interior decorator. My friend and ultramarathoner Reggie O'Hara calls his long runs the "pain-cave," or just "the cave" for short. I liked this image, and imagined my mind as a little mancave. A mancave should be a sanctuary. Over the miles I set about decorating it in a deliberate, intentional way. I covered the walls with motivational posters, with collections of interesting words, with trophies, books, a hall of heroes, and symbols that spoke to me. On one of my hundred mile practice rides, when it rained for sixty of those miles, I sang to myself. The cave has incredible acoustics, and my mind is decorated with the sounds and colors of my thoughts. I learned to be methodical with this self-talk because it is a form of conversation with God, of prayer. Pain helped me to know of my borders and edges of what I could and couldn't do. Pain helped me to know of my mortality and nothingness. Pain helped me to find humility, and that helped me to seek God.

During the semester, during the pain, I started feeling close to God again. I started feeling like I was living the way I was supposed to. I am still afraid, and I still worry about hundreds of things. I renamed my anxious thoughts "restless soul syndrome." Thankfully, over the course of the semester, my restless soul found stillness in motion. In that stillness I worked to make friends with God and with myself.

I thought about how in all of creation, in all the stars and all the trees, there is only one time He has made each of us. And He'll never make another one. The semester helped me realize we were not created to be victims of life. We were not created to be "survivors." We were not created to *find* ourselves. We were created to be creators! And we must work to not just create our understandings of God, but our greatest creations and the best projects we'll ever work on: ourselves. God intends me to develop into the person He put me here to become. He wanted me to contribute to my own creation. And if I want to shape that creation for the better, I have to be willing to embrace discomfort.

I discovered that what I could imagine, I could create. The semester began with a series of ghost-like insights, a vision, followed by a solidifying act of consciously, deliberately creating myself. I wrote out my program, built it around the constraints of my schedule, and the constraints of physical adaptation as I understood them. In the miles through which I ran, biked, and swam, I repeatedly re-created myself. And though He doesn't answer my prayers as clearly and plainly as I would prefer, He does seem to call to me, and forgive me. As Mila Brown said, "I am learning to trust the journey even when I do not understand it." Some people walk by faith, some of us run by faith.

The single biggest area where I needed faith was with death. I struggled with death, with why my grandparents and various patients had died. I remember one day delivering a baby in the morning, seeing some kids and teens in clinic, followed by some young parents and then some retirees. I ended the day at the nursing home, where one of my patients had died. Family medicine let me have days like that where I could watch an entire human life span unfold in one day. Thankfully that patient and her son had been wise about her impending death. It was always so much harder on them and on us, their physicians, when patients struggle with denying their mortality. Charles Bukowski once eloquently said, "We are here to laugh at the odds and live our lives so well that death will tremble to take us."

Tecumseh was right when he added, "When it comes your time to die, be not like those whose hearts are filled with the fear of death, so that when their time comes they weep and pray for a little more time to live their lives over again in a different way. Sing your death song and die like a hero going home."

I imagine at my death being asked what I had done to deserve to enter Heaven.

"I took good care of the body I was given, and in the process inspired a few more people to exercise, to take good care of theirs. I did my best, within the constraints of my own imperfections, to take good care of my patients as I promised God I would if He helped me get into medical school. I also poured the best of myself into loving the delightful wife I was given. I raised a magnificent, disciplined son, and a breathtaking daughter. I left the world a little better than I found it. And I worked to forgive everybody everything. Some of them I had to forgive and not let back into my life, but for my part I forgave them."

I wanted to live a life I could be proud of. I liked to imagine standing before my Maker at the Day of Judgment. In my imagination, when I die all the dogs I have ever loved come with Him to greet me. Dogs always drop what they are doing to welcome us home. They teach us how to live, and they teach us how to die, so I can't imagine any reason why they wouldn't teach us in the next life. When I imagine Judgment Day, I imagine being judged by a perfectly loving jury, so I imagine that is one of dogs' jobs in the next life: to sit on the jury.

I imagine God looking down at me, and me looking up at Him and then smiling at Him with a free conscience, and seeing Him break out into a smile too. Then, I want to reach over and give my God a fist-bump and say, "Wow, life was hard!" and have Him laugh a beautiful laugh with me, and say, "I know it was. And you know what? You were given that life because you were strong enough to live it. Well done. Well done."

And all the dogs will start wagging their tails looking at Him and whimpering. Then, God'll wipe the tears from His merry eyes, and I'll say: "Hey God, do you forgive me for being such an imperfect mess?"

And He'll pause and look at me with a serious look and say: "Do you forgive me for all those patients that died even when you did your best? Do you forgive me for not always answering your prayers in ways that you could understand?"

"Yeah, I'm not gonna lie: that was pretty rough. That's real thoughtful of you to ask." And I'll pause for a minute because I'll be surprised that Judgment Day is a two-way thing. That maybe the only way to get into Heaven is to forgive everyone everything, even God. Then I'll say, "We're still tight. I forgive you God."

And He'll say, "Yeah, me too kid. Me too." And then He'll offer me another fist bump, and after I pound it we'll hug it out the way folks do when they truly and completely forgive each other, when they know that the misunderstanding and pain between them is finally done. Then all the dogs will howl the happy hymn of the heavenly hosts because I'm Home.

Then God will say, "Hey, wanna go for a little jog?" And all the dogs will just go crazy with joy. We'll start jogging with the dogs swarming around us, and my ghostly ancestors will solidify and run with us, just laughing and telling stories, and teasing and explaining. We'll run together and cheer our living descendants to run too. And maybe they'll look up from their runs and exhaustion and sense that they are never running alone.

All my life I have wanted to be friends with God. I have searched for His voice in every area of my life. After squinting with my heart as hard as I can, I finally learned to recognize one of His voices. I believe God speaks to us and calls us with one of the brightest and lightest of voices: curiosity. He called to me as a kid through curiosity about explorers, as a young man I was called on a mission by curiosity. As I young adult, curiosity called me to medicine. He called me out of addiction with curiosity about experimenting with abstinence. I could hear Him calling me to do this crazy semester simply through the whisper of curiosity. And the strange call to study surgery when I am almost forty years old? Curiosity.

And that's the God of my understanding. His traits? He calls us through the things that make us curious. He's funny, and friendly, and forgiving. He's happy when we take good care of our bodies and minds. And He's sorry about the pain in our lives. And He's really sorry about death. Oh, and He loves dogs too. That's the God I believe in, the God I believe created me, and so I returned the compliment. It's a type of story, a type of creation.

And that story leads to my final project of my semester of endurance experiment: writing my thesis.

Do you know the feeling I know?
When your legs have disappeared,
and there is only your heart, your lungs,
and your eyes skimming disembodied through the air?
We are Aristotle's featherless bipeds, we runners.
Though we have no wings,
we have taught ourselves to fly.
Jeff Edmonds, Distance Runner

Change will not come if we wait for some other person,
or some other time.
We are the ones we have been waiting for.
Barack Obama, President

MILE 25
Inveniete Significatium in Passiem

Vemod: (Swedish) (n) a tender sadness or pensive melancholy; the calm feeling that something emotionally significant is over and never will be back.

When I was a missionary in Brazil, a man named Dallas Archibald told a story that changed my life. He said:

"Each morning, on my way to work, I take my teenage daughter to school," he said, "and every morning we had a huge ordeal of me trying to wake her up, so she could get ready and we could leave on time. Well, one morning when we got to the car, it didn't start. So I told her we were going to have to push-start it.

So we got out and started pushing it and pushing it, and then I jumped in and tried to start it, but it didn't start. So we got out and started pushing it again and tried to go even faster this time, and we were working up a real sweat. After it got up to speed, I jumped in and tried to start it, but again, the car didn't start. So, a third time we start pushing it and pushing it, and my poor daughter's make-up was running and her hair was getting matted from the sweat, and when I jumped in, the car started."

"My daughter plops into the seat beside me, panting and sweating, and she turns the air conditioning on full blast. And then I did something that was a little mean," He paused at this point in his story, and then slowly said, "I turned the car off."

"My daughter looks at me with these huge eyes, and says, 'Dad, why did you do that after we worked so hard to get it started?'"

"I looked and her and said, 'Honey, there's something you need to know.' And she blinks at me, and she's still sweating because the air conditioning is off, and I say, 'this car has an automatic starter.' I turn the key and the engine started right up."

"And then I said to her, "Honey, every morning you are like this car, I push you and push you to get ready, and I am exhausted. But I don't need to push you every morning. You have an automatic starter!"

I love that story. It is so easy to forget we all have automatic starters. In life, mediocrity is mandatory. Mandatory things are characterized by the phrase "have to." "I have to run," or "I have to study," or "I have to go to work." This attitude treats our lives like we are just Newtonian solids, waiting for an outside force to act upon us.

But we have automatic starters!

Excellence, in contrast to mediocrity, is voluntary. It represents when we choose to use our automatic starter. It is characterized by the phrase "get to." I get to go to run. I get to push myself. I get to go to school. I get to make the world better. This attitude treats our lives like we are the creators of our own lives, the authors of our own destinies. We act. We are not passively acted upon. The writer Napoleon Hill once said, "Man, alone, has the power to transform his thoughts into physical reality; man, alone, can dream and make his dreams come true." This is because we have automatic starters.

A victim is a person who is acted upon, rather than a self-determining agent who can act for themselves and write their own story, and be a creative creator. I have heard dozens and probably hundreds of patients tell me about how they are the victims of their weight, or the victims of their diabetes, or victims of a rough childhood. One of my favorite posters shows a marine in full dress uniform. Both of his legs are prosthetic. Underneath him it reads: "Regrets? No Mr. President, none that I can think of." This poster is powerful because it shows someone who does not count himself as a victim. We cannot always change the unfortunate events in our lives, but we can choose to change their meaning. This is important: it is not what happens to us that determines our reactions; it is our *interpretation* of those events. We can choose our own interpretations. We can find meaning in suffering. And when it has a meaning, it is no longer suffering. I wanted to go back to residency for the same reasons that soldiers want to go back to war, or why I had done this semester in the first place: because sometimes doing things that might kill you makes you feel strangely alive.

Many times I believe we misinterpret events in our lives. One of the most helpful things we can do to alleviate suffering is to find a different story, a different meaning in it. There are many examples in medicine, but one simple one is the morning sickness associated with pregnancy. If a pregnant woman wakes up with nausea and certain smells make her feel like she will vomit for no reason this can lead to senseless suffering. So she comes in and asks for medicine. The medications we have to treat morning sickness are limited, so now they start to feel like no one can help them. But when we teach these women that those who have worse morning sickness have fewer miscarriages then suddenly the misery has a purpose. Though only partially understood, morning sickness probably happens because their bodies' natural toxin sensors go into overdrive to protect the developing baby during the most vulnerable period of the first trimester when all the organs are developing. Morning sickness is not like the tormenting Furies. It is like the wisdom-giving Eumenides that can teach her she is already being a good mother and protecting her unborn baby.

Viktor Frankl, who focused the pain of surviving the Holocaust to found a new field of psychiatry, wrote a famous book called *Man's Search for Meaning*. In it, he put forth the thesis that in times of suffering we search for meaning. Once we find it, the suffering is transformed. I loved this so much that I based my personal motto on it, "Find Meaning in Suffering." Then, just to make it seem more authentic, my son helped me to translate it into Latin: *Inveniete Significatium in Passiem*, because Latin causes many people suffering and I am a fan of irony. At last I had found my long-awaited Latin logo for my imaginary University of Me sweatshirt.

Too many people treat their fitness (or any of their other dreams) like a teen-age romance: they want gratification but not commitment. They want fitness without the pain and work required to obtain it. Or they miss the point and think they are competing with other people. As Earnest Hemmingway put it, "There is nothing noble in being superior to your fellow man; true nobility is being superior to your former self." The opinions of others are distracting and unimportant. A lion does not concern itself with the opinions of sheep. They miss the point that the training is the *real* race. Training is when we wrestle the most obstacles, the most doubts. If all of those can be overcome, the race is actually easy. The race has excitement, and a cheering crowd. There are measurable miles, other runners, aid stations, and bathrooms! The training is the real race because the training doesn't have a crippling finish line; it only has the promise of an honest struggle to improve.

On its surface, a marathon appears to be 26.2 miles long, but that is not true. To train for my first marathon I ran 461.2 miles. The marathon was just the last 26.2 of these. The practice constituted ninety-five percent of the miles! It was the real thing. During the semester of endurance experiments, the final race was 140.6 miles long, but the semester was 3171.5 miles of training. The training was ninety-five percent of the miles; it was the majority of the whole thing. But even this is a bit of an illusion, a psychological magnification that blows something out of proportion. Though I had to go through every single one of those miles, a mile is just a made up thing. In reality, there is only one footstep in a marathon. It is simply repeated hundreds and hundreds of times. The Semester of Endurance Experiments wasn't just 297.7 miles of races, nor 3171.5 miles of training. It was just one swim stroke, just one circle of the bike pedal, just one more step.

Navy SEALS say that to survive the legendary HELL WEEK, they don't have to survive a week. They just have to make it through one more day. Then as the pain increases they just have to make it until the next meal, then just for one more hour, then just for one more moment. If we can just make it through the hard moment we can make it to the next one. If we can string enough of those together we can do things that we once thought were impossible.

In addiction recovery they teach this same wisdom: we don't have to be sober for the rest of our lives. That is too big, too intimidating. They ask if we can be sober for twenty-four hours. They frame it into a size that our minds can comprehend. There is something about the magnifying powers of our imaginations that distorts things out of proportion if we don't keep them within certain concrete focal lengths.

When it comes to writing a book, John Steinbeck once wrote, "Abandon the idea that you are ever going to finish. Lose track of the four hundred pages and write just one page for each day. It helps. Then when it gets finished, you are always surprised."

I always wanted to learn to play the guitar, but my mind distorted the sheer volume and complexity into something unobtainable. But after this semester, I asked myself if I could learn one string per day. Yes, I could do that. How about one note? Yes, probably. One chord? Yes, that didn't seem difficult. After I strung a few of these together, I was suddenly playing. I still struggle, telling myself that the simple songs I have learned don't count for some reason. I listen politely to these voices, but then tell them that I never said I would play perfectly, but that, yes, I *can* play the guitar.

My grandfather became an engineer without going to college by using this technique to memorize equations and applications.

It does make me wonder, "Could I learn one word of German per day?"

When the semester was over, I sent in my application to go back to residency to study general surgery. After all, wasn't training the real race? My friends at work asked me if I knew what I was doing. My buddy Devin told me it was like watching someone you care about get married to someone you know is wrong for them.

When I interviewed, I was thirty eight years old.

The interviewer looked at me, "You understand this will take five years to complete. Don't you worry about how long that will be?"

I answered, "Well, the five years is really just an illusion."

She looked at me.

"The five years isn't really real. It is really just one patient long. Then another, then another. If I think about all five years, that is like fearing 26.4 miles of a marathon you need to run, or 297.7 pages of a book you need to write. The five years will pass regardless of what I am doing. Earl Nightingale once said, 'Never give up on a dream just because of the time it will take to accomplish it. The time will pass anyway.'"

She made a little note in my file.

I like to imagine that it said, "This curious applicant seems to have an automatic starter, and has figured out how to enjoy doing hard things."

Tears are words that that need to be written.
Paulo Coelho, Author

History will remember me,
and I do not have to worry about him being kind.
I will define myself. I will write my own praises.
John Flowers, Football Coach

MILE 26
An Explorer's Epistle

Alexithymia: (Greek) (n) An inability to describe feelings to other people.

When the Semester of Endurance Experiments was over, the next two semesters at the University of Me were spent writing my thesis: this book. When I was a young kid, I had a fantasy that I would one day discover a leather-bound journal of an adventurer, probably filled with some treasure maps and tips for how to impress girls and other acts of bravery, but most importantly with a plea for whoever found it to continue with the quest.

I once asked my father if there were any places left to explore, anything new to discover. I wanted to be swallowed in the awesomeness of nature, to see new animals and taste new things. When he said there weren't, I felt my boyhood dreams and sense of wonder being crushed under reality's boot heel. But Ayn Rand reminds us: "Do not let the hero in your soul perish in lonely frustration for the life you deserved and have never been able to reach."

When I was a young kid, I decided that I would try to learn and master the skills of being an adventurer, or an explorer. And so, at the end of this semester of explorations, I thought I would write a letter of encouragement back to that little me of my past with some tips, some rules to guide me going forward:

Dear Young Sir,

It has come to my attention that you have a budding interest in being an explorer and/or adventurer. As you know, the great exploration—the journey to adventure—goes by many names. In the books you have studied it was sometimes a labyrinth, an abyss, a strange foreign country, dark forest, or a voyage through night or winter. Contemporarily, it is sometimes called a 'walkabout,' a vision quest, a sabbatical, or a pilgrimage. Though he was cartographically correct and just being honest with you, your father probably misunderstood your question about if there were any places left to explore. Forgive him. You were trying to find the path to what the Sufi mystic Rumi once called the "long journey into yourself." Remember as you embark on your own adventures, we don't explore to escape from life, but rather to keep life from escaping from us.

I have collected, for your benefit, "Eight Edicts for Explorers:"

First: Curiosity is the Explorer's Compass. It leads us to our passions, our callings, and ourselves. When we stop being curious we stop exploring.

My daughter told me one night, "Dad, you know when you aren't sure how something works, and then you learn and it is actually way better than you imagined?"

"Yes Squashy."

"Well, that just blows my mind. And I really, really like that feeling when my mind is blown."

Curiosity is the fuse that burns to find those things that blow our minds. If we follow the paths to which curiosity directs us, then we find the greatest of treasures: newer, better versions of ourselves! The philosopher Lao Tzu taught us, "At the center of your being you have the answer; you know who you are and you know what you want." That center pulls the needle of our curiosity's compass. Trust it.

Second: Make Friends with Yourself. Friends forgive, admire, gently correct, tease, and celebrate each other. You have to get comfortable living inside your own skin, your own legs and your own mind. Your thoughts were not wild animals from which you need to escape, but they do occasionally need to be domesticated.

For example, when I set out to compile my field notes on my adventure, a familiar voice of self doubt cleared its phlegmy throat and asked:

"Who are you to write a book? What do you have to say? You'll never say something new or original or profound or true. It will never be a best-seller, or critically reviewed, it will never be good enough."

To which I gently replied (it is most important to use a gentle voice when domesticating wild things), "I never said it would be those things, I only said I was going to write it."

Sometimes the people around you won't understand your story, or your explorations. They don't need to. Your explorations aren't for them; they are for you, the explorer. Do not be afraid to become an athlete/writer/explorer of your own making. Believe in the person you want to become. Douglas Adams once wrote, "I may not have gone where I intended to go, but I think I have ended up where I intended to be."

Third: Adventure and Comfort are Inversely Related. There is no adventure in sitting someplace comfortably. Adventures are physically uncomfortable. Therefore, work to inoculate your body against discomfort. Become a student of discomfort. Get familiar with it, both its smooth curves, and its sharp edges. Practice being in its company often. Your body becomes strong only through the discomfort of exercise. Your mind only becomes strong through the discomfort of study and being corrected by teachers. Your spirit only becomes strong through the discomfort of humbly seeking God. Get comfortable with being uncomfortable.

Fourth: Learn the Rules. Look for the underlying laws, patterns, and connections that shape the way your own mind, the minds of other people, animals, your body, nature, your own family, God and the universe work. To tease out the rules, do experiments. Mendel discovered the rules of genetics by paying attention. Newton discovered so much of the laws of physics by paying attention. I discovered these rules for being an adventurer by paying attention this way. There are probably more of them that I haven't discovered yet. Do some experiments and find them!

Fifth: Live your life as a series of obsessions. My friend Trent Elliott calls this having a "focus." The mind of an explorer is supposed to be multifocal. Build the University of Yourself, and plan and design your own curricula.

Attract what you expect,
Reflect what you desire,
Become what you respect,
Mirror what you admire.

When the races of my adventure were over, my wife gave me a present. It was small, and light, and flat. I opened it. In it there were nine bumper stickers that read: 0.0, 5k, 10k, 13.2, 26.4, 38.6, 50, 70.3, and 140.6. I remembered the photo of the bumper that had started it all. We put them on my car. It wasn't to brag to anyone else. It was to remind myself, and my demons. It was to put a stopper in some of the holes in my heart that love drained out of. Some may think that having a car with those bumper stickers would be arrogant. But when I had first seen them in a photo years ago I found them absolutely inspiring. I wanted to mirror what I admired.

Sixth: Everything is Interesting. You must open your eyes. You must see the wonders around you. Then, you must look closer and like a good explorer, you must take field notes! Susan Sontag noted "A writer is someone who pays attention to the world." Writing will help you to step back and to look and to notice the stories going on around you, and inside your own mind. Even your own doubts, fears, anger, and pain are interesting. As you figure out how to describe what you are feeling, it will help to separate the feeling from being so personal. Fatigue can simply become something interesting to try to describe, instead of something dreaded to feel. Writing can make new things feel familiar, and familiar things feel new.

Many times you will have a good idea and tell yourself you will remember it, but it will slip away. Because of their fragility, if an insight strikes you in the middle of an expeditionary run, chant it to yourself as you run so you do not forget. Sadly, even good ideas are not always sticky, or maybe it is just that our minds are naturally slippery. After you return from your explorations, jot down notes of the thoughts that ran through your mind. Think of your pen as a lightning rod: useful for capturing ideas when they unexpectedly strike. Carry one, and take notes when inspiration strikes. If you don't pay attention to your muse, it will take the insights to someone who will. When ideas struck me, I wrote them on little pieces of paper, on index cards, on post-its and in my journal. I collected them and organized them, and thought I was saving them from extinction, when in fact they will probably save me from such a fate when I am gone. Books are thoughts that got captured, words that got stuck when the thoughts struck. Also, when writing the story of your adventures and life, please do not let anyone else hold the pen.

Seventh: Chronicle your Adventures: WRITE! We have to write because explorers write about their adventures. This is one of the ways we use the flame of inspiration to kindle wonder in young explorers. We have to write in order to slow down time to a speed where we can actually see wonders unfold because frequently they happen so quickly. Edward P. Morgan pointed out "A book is the only place in which you can examine a fragile thought without breaking it, or explore an explosive idea without fear it will go off in your face. It is one of the few havens remaining where a man's mind can get both provocation and privacy." The pen is a weapon of mass creation. The stories we tell ourselves create ourselves. Writing is one of the means by which we can transform our lives from the mundane into the mythical. Be thoughtful about making the mythology of your own life, and adventures.

Remember what Nobel Laureate Toni Morrison famously said, "If there's a book that you want to read, but it hasn't been written yet, then you must write it." And Junot Diaz added, "In order to write the book you want to write, in the end you have to become the person you need to become to write that book." You have to live the life you would want to read about.

If you learn to write, you will learn to think. If you learn to write well, you will learn to think well. So study words. Collect them. Patti Hill described how difficult it is to find the right words to describe our thoughts when she said that "writing… is like wrestling an octopus into a mayonnaise jar." As writers, wrestle we must, but it is much easier when we have a good collection of both wrestling moves and potential jars.

As a run is done step by step and mile by mile, a book is done word by word, page by page, and chapter by chapter.

Erica Jong warned us, "All writing problems are psychological problems. Blocks usually stem from the fear of being judged. If you imagine the world listening, you'll never write a line. That's why privacy is so important. You should write first drafts as if they will never be shown to anyone."

When I think of my first marathon and how I had to train privately on a treadmill in my basement I agree. When I think of my grandfather, running laps through the privacy of his house in his underwear, I thought, "All fitness problems are psychological problems. Fitness blocks usually stem from fear of being judged. If you imagine the world watching and judging, you'll never jog a mile. That is why privacy is so important. You should run the first mile as if it will never be shown to anyone."

Steven Pressfield reminds us that "If you find yourself asking yourself (and your friends) 'am I really a writer? Am I really an artist?' chances are you are. The counterfeit innovator is wildly self confident. The real one is scared to death." Again, the word "athlete," or "runner," or "explorer" can be substituted.

To write is to be vulnerable. To run is to be vulnerable. To love another person is to be vulnerable. To explore something new is to be vulnerable. Being vulnerable is part of being courageous. Your life is your message to the world; ensure that you make it courageous and inspiring!

In conclusion, if you wish to lead an adventurous life—one bursting with other fascinating explorers, with music, leather-bound journals filled with elegant penmanship and sepia sketches, adoring animal sidekicks, mouth-watering foods, secret-passages, athletic freaks for friends, majestic words, a fit body worthy of admiration, a feeling of peace with nature, heart-stopping romance, a true friendship with God, life and death decisions, legends and incredible stories—then you must surround yourself precisely with those things! When you cultivate beauty around yourself, you give your own soul the nutrients, and the sanctuary it needs to flourish. Everything in your life builds or destroys these dreams: what you do, how you dress, where you travel, the books you read, the websites you visit, the people you allow into your life, the God you believe in. If you want to be a marathoner be a marathoner! If you want to be a writer, be a writer! If you want to be a surgeon, be a surgeon!

I will conclude my epistle with my favorite quote of all time. Marianne Williamson said, "Our deepest fear is not that we are inadequate. Our deepest fear is that we are powerful beyond measure. It is our light, not our darkness that most frightens us. We ask ourselves, who am I to be brilliant, gorgeous, talented and fabulous? Actually who are you *not* to be? You are a child of God. Your playing small does not serve the world. There is nothing enlightened about shrinking so that other people will not feel insecure around you. We are all meant to shine, as children do. We were born to make manifest the glory of God that is within us. It is not just in some of us; it is in everyone and as we

287

let our own light shine, we unconsciously give others permission to do the same. As we are liberated from our own fear, our presence automatically liberates others."

When you were a young kid, you once asked if there were any places left to explore. I just wanted you to know there are many, many unexplored and uncharted places desperately in need of explorers. Just in case you know of someone who might be interested in an adventure…

My best wishes on your explorations!

I am very truly yours,

T.A.Stephensen

Appendix

The Plan

Finifugal: (Old English) (adj) hating endings; of someone who tries to avoid or prolong the final moments of a story, relationship, or some other journey.

Because people have asked for the actual nuts and bolts of how I did the semester, I thought I would include my charts. I want people to run, and I want to remove any barriers, including mystery. Initially when I designed this program, it was based loosely on other training regimens, and then adapted to my own schedule, time constraints, and decision that I would not run on the Sabbath. When I first designed these, there was a column for the sum total miles that week, as well as one for the percent increase. I tried to keep the percent increase around ten percent and found that my body was able to adapt at that rate. However, sometimes I was not able to complete everything that was originally planned due to other things I needed to get to on those days. The following week I continued on with the mileage I had planned, but it led to some dips in mileage at times.

Feel free to use these as a reference, but they probably won't work perfectly for you.

Remember to run your own race.

My Four Day a Week Marathon Training Plan							
Wk	Sun	Mon	Tues	Wed	Thur	Fri	Sat	Sum
1		3	3		3		6	15
2		3	3		3		7	16
3		3	4		3		5	15
4		3	4		3		9	19
5		3	5		3		10	21
6		3	5		3		7	18
7		3	6		3		12	24
8	REST DAY	3	6	REST DAY	3	REST DAY	13	25
9		3	7		4		10	24
10		3	7		4		15	29
11		4	8		4		16	32
12		4	8		4		12	28
13		4	9		5		18	36
14		5	9		5		14	33
15		5	10		5		20	40
16		5	8		4		12	29
17		4	6		3		8	21
18		3	5		2		**26.2**	36

It goes without saying, but this chart presumes that you can already run about five miles when you start it. If you can't, just dial it back to the mileage you can run.

Wk	Sun	Mon	Tues	Wed	Thurs	Fri	Sat	Sum
36.8 Mile Ultramarathon Training Plan 1								
1		1	3.5	1	3	1	5	14.5
2		1	3.5	1	3	1.5	7	17
3		1.5	3.5	1	3		9	18
4		1	3.5	1	4		11	20.5
5		1.5	4	1	4		13	23.5
6		1	4	1.5	4		15	25.5
7	REST DAY	1.5	5	1	4	1	17	29.5
8		5		6	0	20		31
9		6		6	0	13		24.5
10		3.5	6		5		26	40.5
11			4		5		28	37
12			6		6		30	42
13			4		4		15	23
14		6	1	6			**37**	49.8

36.8 Mile Ultramarathon Training Plan II

Wk	Sun	Mon	Tue	Wed	Thu	Fri	Sat
1		BIKE 24	2		3		13
2		BIKE 24	4	BIKE 24	3		13
3		BIKE 24	5	BIKE 24	4	REST	13
4		BIKE 24	6	BIKE 24	6		14
5		BIKE 24	6	BIKE 24	4		15
6		BIKE 24	5	BIKE 24	6	2	17
7		BIKE 24	6	BIKE 24	4	2	19
8	REST	BIKE 24	6	BIKE 24	0	0	20
9		BIKE 24	8	BIKE 24	7		17
10		BIKE 24	6	BIKE 24		20	0
11		BIKE 24	6	BIKE 24	0	26	0
12		BIKE 24	5	BIKE 24	8		23
13		BIKE 24	6	BIKE 24	22	REST	28
14		BIKE 24	11	BIKE 24	6		30
15		BIKE 24	6	BIKE 24	22		10
16		BIKE 24	6	BIKE 24			**37**

50 Mile Ultramarathon Plan						
Wk	Sun	Mon	Tue	Wed	Thu	Fri	Sat
17		6	6	BIKE 24			
18		16	0	BIKE 24		22	BIKE 24
19		6	11	BIKE 24		22	11.5
20	REST DAY	3	0	BIKE 24	REST DAY	6	26
21		BIKE 24 RUN 6	6	BIKE 24		6	20
22		BIKE 24	11	BIKE 24		4	10
23		BIKE 24	6	BIKE 24		0	50

I was not pleased with the results I got for the fifty mile run. Looking at these charts, I actually was running fewer miles training for that race than I had in training for the 36.8 mile run. Various forums had recommended doing back-to-back long runs in training, rather than single monster long runs to avoid injuries. If I get to do that one over again, I would probably do some sort of hybrid, where I did back-to-back long runs, but I'd probably have my Saturday long run longer, over thirty miles at least, maybe over thirty-five miles. I'll have to experiment with it…

		1/2 Ironman Plan					
Wk	Sun	Mon	Tue	Wed	Thu	Fri	Sat
24		Bk 24			Bk 50		Sw 30 Bk 35 Rn 11
25		Bk 35 Sw 45	Rn 22	Bk 24 Sw 60		Bk 24 Rn 1	Sw 30 Bk 50 Rn 13
26	REST DAY	Bk 35 Sw 90	Rn 22	Bk 24 Sw 60	Bk 15	Bk 24 Sw 60	Sw 90 Bk 50 Rn 15
27		Bk 24 Rn 8	Rn 22	Bk 24 Sw 60	Bk 15	Bk 24 Rn 3	Sw 120 Bk 50 Rn 15
28		Bk 24 Rn 9	Rn 9	Bk 24 Sw 60	REST		Sw 60 Bk 56 Rn 13

Key:
Bk = Bike, the number is miles
Sw = Swim, the number is in MINUTES
Rn = Run, the number is miles

				Full Ironman Plan			
Wk	Sun	Mon	Tue	Wed	Th	Fri	Sat
29	REST DAY		R 20 S 60	B 50	REST DAY	B 24 S120	S 120 B 50 R 15
30		B 50 S 60	R 22	B 24 S 60		B 24 S 120	S 180 B 80 R 18
31		B 50 S 60	R 22	B 24 S 60		B 24 S 120	S 180 B 100 R 20
32		B 50 S 60	R 22	B 24 S 60		B 24 S 120	S 180 B 112 R 20
33		B 50		B 24 S 60			S 120 B 112 R 26

Key:

B = Bike, the number is miles
S = Swim, the number is in MINUTES
R = Run, the number is miles

ABOUT THE AUTHOR

Travis Stephensen is the descendent of a long line of curious people, and a future ancestor of even more curious people. Once upon a time he founded a university, spent a semester racing 297.7 miles and wrote a book with a page dedicated to each mile. His first book was banned. He is currently working on a book about surgical residency.